# Son of a Son of a Gambler

Winners, Losers, and What to
Do When You Win the Lottery:
A World with Gamblers,
Kentuckians, Addicts,
Cincinnati, Al Gore, Larry Flynt,
and the Scissor Sisters

—Don McNay—

ISBN 978-0-9793644-0-2

Book cover designed by:
Janet Long
jlong@eaze.net

1.0

*To my father, Joe McNay, my mother Ollie McNay
and my sister Theresa McNay-Francis.*

*Somewhere in heaven, my father is telling funny stories, my sister is bragging on her children and my mother is waiting for the day when Tom Jones shows up.*

*Everything in this book should be historically accurate. However, my father liked to embellish and was a primary source of information. Thus, the opening line of the movie,* The Life and Times of Judge Roy Beam *shall serve as a disclaimer.*

*"If it is not the way it was, it is the way it should have been."*

# Table of Contents

# Section Nine: Financial Rip-offs and Soldiers..............................265

# Section Ten: Credit Cards and Other Sucker Bets.......................................279

# Section Eleven: Winners and Losers in the Worlds of Addiction.........309

# INTRODUCTION

*"Read dozens of books about heroes and crooks; yes, I learned much from both of their styles."*

**—Jimmy Buffett, "Son of a Son of a Sailor," 1978**

I've met a lot of heroes and crooks.

If my childhood had been filmed as a reality series, we would have beaten the Sopranos in the ratings.

Before there was a modern Las Vegas, there was Northern Kentucky. That's where I grew up. The area was controlled by mobsters. My father, like his father before him, made his bones working in the bingo halls, bars and gambling joints of Covington and Newport.

When the gangsters were run out of town in the 1960's, dad started his own gambling enterprises. He eventually went legit and did well in the travel business.

I was surrounded by colorful people, but I didn't know they were colorful.

I thought everyone had names like "Peanuts," "Lucky," "Jelly," and "Screen Door Smitty."

I moved away for college and never came back. I got into the worlds of money and personal finance. Now I specialize in helping people who receive settlements and large lump sums.

My father's world was the mean streets, and my world is one of lawyers, actuaries, and financiers.

Those worlds collided at dad's 1993 funeral.

As they were getting ready to take his coffin down the aisle of the church, a prosecutor friend asked to talk to me. I told him I was busy. He got in my face and said "Don, I need to talk to you *now!*"

He pointed across the church and said, "Don, who is *that?*"

They had seated my friend behind a fellow we'll call "Stun-Gun." That is not the man's real name or nickname. I don't want to wear a cement overcoat, so that is as much information as you will get.

"Stun-Gun" was a reputed mobster in a major city. You could tell he was a reputed mobster from 100 yards away. He and my dad vacationed and shot craps together.

My prosecutor friend had overheard "Stun-Gun" say, "I hope the FBI doesn't have the pews wired. . . . If God sees who is in this church, the walls are going to come crumbling down."

Many of my friends had been in a church, but for dad's friends, it was a maiden voyage.

My world and my father's world meet at many junctures.

Dad was a gambler and I have helped lottery winners with their finances.

You won't read stories about my clients in the papers. I do everything to keep who they are confidential. My father said never to "flash your roll" in public and it is good advice.

In this book, you'll read about some lottery "losers" who went public and probably regret it.

I'll tell you not to play the lottery, but give you some pointers—in case you ignore my advice and then hit the jackpot.

People in dad's world had problems with addictions and money. People in my world have those problems too.

The rich and famous have passed through our lives. Dad's friends were local Cincinnati celebrities and a Kentuckian who made it big in pornography, Larry Flynt.

I spent time with rockers like the Scissor Sisters and politicians like Al Gore.

I love rock and roll and start each of my newspaper columns with a rock lyric to set the theme.

I compare this book to "concept" albums like the Eagles' *Hotel California*, The Beatles' *Sergeant Pepper's Lonely Hearts Club Band*, and Meat Loaf's *Bat out of Hell*. The albums each had a wide range of songs, but all of them tied back to the album's central theme.

In this book, I touch a variety of topics that all go back to the same idea.

So, to borrow from Jimmy Buffett, you could say my theme, and my reality, is that I'm the son of the son of a gambler.

# Section One
# Lottery Winners

# What to Do When You Win the Lottery

I tell everyone that buying lottery tickets is a bad idea.

If you ignore my advice, play anyway and win the big jackpot, this advice is for you.

You would think that after having overcome trillion-to-one odds, the idea of running through millions of dollars would seem silly. Studies reportedly show that 90% of lottery winners blow all their money within five years of winning the jackpot.

I have counseled some lottery winners. Here are a few tips I have given them:

### 1. Never let anyone know you won.
Every lottery winner who goes public eventually reports that they have had people harassing them.

Powerball winner Jack Whittaker said, "There should be a book to tell you how to handle it when people get thrown into the limelight."

You are asking for trouble if you have a news conference and tell the world that you have a bunch of money that you never planned on having.

The news conference is good for the lottery officials promoting their product, and it provides a good story for the media. It will not, however, turn out so well for you.

Bowling Green, Kentucky attorney Steve Thornton announced a few years ago that one of his clients had won the Kentucky lottery. Steve set up a corporation and protected the client's identity.

If you win the lottery, find someone who can give you the same privacy. Your life will be much happier. If you decide that you want to be famous, you will have enough money to fund your own reality show.

### 2. *Take the annual payments, not the lump sum.*

Never take a lump sum. The annual payments are a better deal.

Lottery winners are totally unprepared for sudden wealth.

If you take the money as a lump sum, and are overcome by lust, drugs, sex, bad friends, bad family, bad investments, or other factors, then the money will be gone, and there will be no way to get it back.

If you take annual payments and run through the first check, you have twenty-nine more chances to get it right. It gives you time to organize a plan and take advantage of ways to save taxes and improve return.

Even if you ignored my advice and bought a lottery ticket, listen to me on this one.

### 3. Spend money on some good advice.

There are a ton of tax breaks for the wealthy. When you win the lottery, you need to find advisors who can get those tax breaks for you.

Getting good advice does not mean calling the book-keeper for your bowling league. You need someone who has dealt with big money and is not trying to learn while they earn.

Big-time advisors do not advertise in the phone book under "Help for Lottery Winners," but if you ask some well-respected attorneys, you will eventually get referred to the kind of advisor you need.

There are people who are good at helping rich people become richer; get one of them working for you.

### 4. Use your money for a purpose.

There was a great book written in the 1980's by Ami Domini called *The Challenges of Wealth*. It was a groundbreaking study of sudden wealth written during a time when few studies were available on the subject.

Her research showed that rich people are happiest when they help a cause that they really believe in. The most joyful people were those who gave money for scholarships, helped their church, and formed non-profit groups.

You can leave your children enough money to be comfortable without spoiling them. People who leave their families too much money wind up with children like Paris Hilton.

If you study history, you will find that most of the people who amassed great fortunes, like Carnegie and Rockefeller, gave substantial amounts of money to charity while they were still alive. Even more gave money to charity upon death.

You have an opportunity to take care of family and have plenty left over to make an impact on society. It will make you content and make the world a better place.

### *One last thought:*

Winning the lottery is a random event. It has nothing to do with skill, hard work, or talent.

If you ever start feeling cocky about your brains and good fortune, remember that I told you not to buy the ticket in the first place.

# A Trust Can Make Life a Dance for a Lottery Winner

*"Life's a dance you learn as you go; sometimes you lead, sometimes you follow."*

**—John Michael Montgomery**

For years, I have been giving advice to lottery winners. Usually, the advice is ignored, and people learn as they go.

Now someone has followed my advice.

Someone purchased a lottery ticket near Cincinnati and won a $148.1 million jackpot. They did not claim the money themselves.

Instead, they set up a trust at a bank and had the bank's trust officer cash the winning ticket.

The trust officer was prohibited from giving out the name of the winner, as was the lottery commission. No one knows who or where the winner is.

The winner eliminated many problems with one smart decision.

Almost all lottery winners rush to the lottery office the second they figure out that they have won.

They often have a news conference where they jump up and down like participants on a television game show; not Jeopardy, but one of those shows where you don't need to be smart.

These new millionaires get their "professional" financial advice from newfound family and friends.

These new advisors often have other careers as strippers and bartenders which explains why an estimated 90% of lottery winners run through the money in less than five years.

I tell winners not to have a news conference, but they have it anyway. They can't resist the chance to be on television and impress people with their intelligence and good intentions.

Although it does not take a rocket scientist to randomly pick numbers, winners seemed compelled to show off their special prowess.

Since flashing money in public is a sure sign that you are an idiot, one can see why con artists go after lottery winners.

The winners universally say that they are going to help their families and give money to charities.

Winners must have family members and charities related to booze and the sex and narcotics industries, as that is where a lot of lottery money seems to go. My bet is that only about 10% of the winners actually give money to benefit society.

The rest blow their money being stupid.

I tell people not to have news conferences and to get a professional financial advisor. I also tell people not to play the lottery at all.

Millions of people ignore my advice.

The winner in Cincinnati acted as if they had listened to me. WLW radio in Cincinnati has had me on several times; maybe they heard me.

Since we don't know who the winners are, they are not going to come forward and give me credit. So I will take credit for it anyway. If they did not listen to me, they listened to someone who knew what they were doing.

My one argument would have been their decision to take payments from the lottery in a lump sum instead of payments over thirty years. Payments over time are usually a better tax and financial planning strategy.

About 98% of lottery winners ignore me, but it is good advice anyway.

I shouldn't knock the strategy of the unknown winner because the trust is a great tool.

Restrictions can be set up, and with good management, the money could be in their family for generations to come.

The winner has a shot at maintaining wealth, since no one will know that they have it. They will miss the thrill of acting stupid in public, but it is a great trade off. They won't have charities and leeches harassing them. They won't have the opportunity to establish "deep" bonding experiences with long lost friends and relatives.

Instead, they will enjoy the money in private. If they feel compelled to go to a strip bar and flash a few hundred thousand, as West Virginia Powerball winner Jack Whitaker liked to do, they can pretend that they actually earned the money

Keeping quiet is the first advice I give anyone getting a large amount of money, be it from the lottery, an injury settlement, or an inheritance.

A large lump sum is a one-time experience, and most people either learn or don't learn as they go.

Their lives should be a dance, not a fire walk.

# Taming the Lottery Tiger

*"I've got a tiger by the tail; it's plain to see; I won't be much when you get through with me."*

**—Buck Owens**

When Buck Owens died, tributes were made to his great musical skills. Few knew that Buck was also a disciplined businessman. He owned television and radio stations and was a sharp investor.

I doubt Buck ever stood in line to buy lottery tickets.

The lottery can be the worst thing that ever happened to both lottery winners and lottery losers.

I hate the lottery. I hate the big Powerball jackpots with a zillion to one odds. I hate watching winners completely screw up their lives like Jack Whitaker did.

I hate standing in line watching people buy instant winner tickets. There is a thrill to instant winner tickets that absolutely escapes me.

I can see spending a dollar on a chance to be super rich. I can't see what attracts people to win two dollars and then give it back to the clerk to buy two more dollars worth of tickets; especially as I wait in line behind them.

I hate watching people be exploited by those who run lotteries. People go on television with an oversized check and expose their lives to the public. I hate the media making celebrities out of people who happened to pick a lucky number.

The winners are not role models. They were just lucky. Every time someone wins a lottery, the media should black out the faces of the winners and run a story about someone who built their own business, or someone who helped to make the world better.

It would be better for society and better for the lottery winners too.

Building a business takes hard work and talent. Even inheriting wealth requires good genetics. Most people who inherit money have time to plan for their eventual fortune.

Lottery winners receive their money suddenly and are thrown into a media circus.

I hate the television interviews that lottery winners give. The winners always have reasonable sounding goals, like paying off their mortgage or educating their children. They never mention booze and strip joints.

They might be serious about doing something good with their money. It is just that temptation, greedy friends, and bad advice get in the way.

When you get financial planning advice from bartenders and strippers, things can get lost in translation.

I always recommend that lottery winners not take the money in a lump sum and not tell anyone they won.

The lottery organizers came up with a game I almost like. It is called "Win for Life."

In "Win for Life," the winner gets a $1000 a week ($52,000 a year) for the rest of their lives. They are guaranteed a $1 million payout.

It is the same kind of "structured settlement" concept that works for helping injured people.

Giving someone $1000 a week will improve their life-style but will not cause freeloaders and hucksters to knock down their door. If a person blows $1000, they get another $1000 the next week and have the rest of their lives to get it right.

I liked the Win for Life idea so much that I thought about buying a ticket. Then I looked at the odds.

The odds of actually "winning for life" are 5,200,000 to one.

I will hang on to my dollar.

Although I love the concept, I suspect Win for Life will not be successful. Lottery players either want huge jackpots or the immediate gratification that instant games provide.

Lotteries are many people's "Tiger by the Tail."

*The biggest winners in the lottery are not those who buy the tickets. The ultimate big winner is someone who can buy their own lottery.*

# Buying Your Own Lottery: A Comeback for Robber Barons

**"Yes, I am a pirate; two hundred years too late; cannons don't thunder; there is nothing to plunder."**

**—Jimmy Buffett**

Jimmy Buffett's character in the song "A Pirate Looks at 40" laments the fact that he missed the era of high-seas piracy.

Like Buffett's "pirate," there are modern businesspeople who wish they were living in the time of industrial "robber barons."

Now those wannabes could get their chance. With proposals to privatize state lotteries, 21st century robber barony may be ripe for a comeback.

Nineteenth-Century robber barons had their gains subsidized by the government. They were given land, inside deals, and special considerations that made it impossible to lose money. In return, the robber barons cycled money back to politicians in the form of bribes, gifts, and campaign contributions.

The "money for favors" cycle has been around since time immemorial, but no one put it into practice like the robber barons. In a time when railroad construction put huge money on the table for government officials, there was always plenty to steal and pass around.

Everyone was happy except for the taxpayers.

I thought the robber barons might have gone the way of pirates until the story broke about the state of Illinois wanting to sell its lottery to private owners.

Illinois wants roughly $10 billion for the lottery. If I can scrape up the $10 billion and get connected to the right politicians, I want to buy it. There is no way to lose.

Most businesses start with a dream, a prayer, and then a test in an unknown market. In this case, however, Illinois has already done the testing. Whoever buys the lottery has a monopoly, stable market, steady players, and the benefit of advertising paid for by Illinois taxpayers. That's a pretty good deal.

Since Illinois politicians are giving away their future for a one-time payoff, there will be a lot of interested buyers. Don't be surprised if potential buyers throw a few dollars the politicians' way. There is too much at stake to not want an inside edge.

I wish the great Chicago columnist Mike Royko had lived to see the lottery sale. It's a story he would have loved to have written about. Not only will there be potential buyers currying favor, there will also be a ton of people who want a piece of the $10 billion dollars brought in by the sale.

Illinois politicians will feel like Scarlett O' Hara at the big barbeque. They will be wined, dined, and courted.

Even if the lottery sale can be done on the up and up, it is still a terrible idea.

Illinois will eventually have to raise taxes or cut services to compensate for the income that was once generated by the lottery.

I worry about private industry managing a lottery. Private owners will market it in ways that governments would not. The purchasing company will seek the quickest way to boost profits—exploiting the poor.

The Illinois lottery can't sell tickets near welfare offices. A private owner will. People will blow their family's welfare money before they get off the block.

Before states made them legitimate, lotteries had a different name: the numbers racket.

The crime lords who ran them made an incredible amount of money, just like the states are making now.

State-run lotteries took the stigma away from the numbers racket.

You will see huge corporations looking to a buy a lottery. What will happen when these companies are managed by the same people who managed Enron?

If the corporations go broke, do lottery winners get stiffed, or does the state of Illinois jump in and guarantee the payments? If so, they may need to take in more than $10 billion.

Mafia-fronted businesses are always interested in gaming. States will need to be extra careful to keep them out of the private lottery business.

The mob has their own way of ensuring profitability. The numbers racket in my hometown was run by a guy named Frank "Screw" Andrews. At some point, Screw's business came into question. Shortly thereafter, he "accidentally" fell out of a fourth-floor window.

Selling the lottery might fund great programs if states spend the money wisely, and robber barons, mobsters, and greedy corporations are kept at bay.

I would take the other side on that bet.

With billions of lottery dollars to plunder, my bet is on pirates and robber barons making a big comeback.

# Section Two
# Lottery Losers

# *Powerball Jack: The Ultimate Lottery Loser*

*I had originally planned on devoting an entire book to Jack Whittaker and other "lottery losers" who hit the big jackpot and had their lives go to hell.*

*I decided against it since it seemed like I was writing the same story over and over again. As I note in the story of David Edwards, newspapers could save money by using a "fill in the blanks" news story about Powerball winners who get into trouble.*

*Since Jack Whittaker won the biggest jackpot, it seems he would have been a prime candidate for the biggest pitfalls.*

*The following are some parts of his weird and twisted saga.*

# Jack Whittaker: Lottery Loser

Some people think money will make them happy. That is the reason they keep buying lottery tickets. The odds of winning are about a trillion to one. They are looking for a quick answer to life's problems.

Winning the lottery brings a whole new list of problems.

Take the case of Jack Whittaker, the West Virginia man who was the biggest lottery winner ever. In 2002, Whitaker took home over $100 million from the Powerball.

Usually you read about millionaires on the business page. Jack made regular appearances in another part of the paper, the police blotter.

Jack needed his own police force or possibly a private army. Bad things kept happening to him.

While he was hanging out at a strip club, someone put a drug in his drink and took $545,000 that he had in his truck. He was charged with threatening a bartender and groping a waitress, and an 18-year-old was found dead in his house.

I've spent my life helping people with large amounts of money. The people who cope do two things: they don't take the money in a lump sum, and they don't brag about how much money they have.

I'm convinced lotteries offer payments over time only to make the jackpot look larger. The lotteries can then advertise the ultimate payout rather than the "cash option" payment that they know people are going to take.

Jack violated both of my rules. He took the "cash option" and let the whole world know that he had money.

If you get a lot of money, never tell anyone about it; you are asking for trouble if you do.

Getting a lump sum gave him problems he never planned on having.

No one knows they are going to win the lottery so they don't have plans for what to do with the winnings. Jack had two decisions and he messed up both. He should have taken the money over time and kept quiet about it.

He won the biggest jackpot but became another lottery loser.

# Jack Whittaker: The Worst That Could Happen

*"Maybe it's the best thing; maybe it's the best thing for you; but it's the worst that could happen to me."*

—Jimmy Webb

Some people believe winning the lottery would be best thing for them; not Jack Whittaker. Winning the Powerball jackpot was the worst thing that could have happened to him.

Before he won the lottery, Jack did not have a bad life. He was making good money as a contractor in West Virginia, and he had been married to the same woman for forty years. He was close to his teenage granddaughter.

Jack's life became hell after winning the lottery. He kept getting arrested for drunk driving and getting robbed in strip clubs. He and his wife divorced, and his granddaughter died of a drug overdose.

His wife wished that they had torn up the winning ticket.

Stories like Jack's are frequent, and they can't be good publicity for lotteries. The winners become marks for every con artist.

I wonder if the people running lotteries think about people like Jack. The lottery gets a ton of free publicity when someone wins, and lottery web pages run stories about how winners plan to give money to charity.

Lotteries skip over the part about winners blowing money on booze, strippers, and drugs, even though that happens much more than winners giving money to the United Way.

A lottery web page says the average lottery player has at least a high school education and makes between $25,000 and $35,000 a year.

That particular "study" overlooked the lottery players in the stores that I go to. The people I see who play the lottery don't seem to be well-educated, big-money types; especially when they are counting out pennies in order to buy a ticket.

If I were on a lottery board, things would definitely change.

Since I have written several columns bashing the lottery, I doubt I'll see my name on the list of gubernatorial appointments.

In fact, I have a better chance of winning the lottery than getting appointed to run it.

The lottery board should be working on ways to protect winners from becoming losers, like what happened to Jack.

The board could do two things that would make life better: they could eliminate the cash option, and they could refuse to release the names of the winners.

The lottery board engages in false advertising, claiming that the lottery jackpot is $100 million, when the cash option payout is only half of that. The people in charge of the lottery know that almost everyone takes the cash option.

By eliminating the cash option, people would then have a chance to get adjusted to living with big money. If they ran through all their money in a year, they would have another opportunity to handle it better the next year and the years after that.

People are used to receiving money in weekly or monthly payments. To give them a lump sum with no preparation invites disaster.

The lottery board gets great press when they publicize the winner and present them with a big check. Unfortunately, things aren't so great for the person holding the check.

I work with many injured people, and most of the settlements are confidential. Sometimes word gets out, and it is horrible to see what it does to families and friendships. Every person with a sad story suddenly feels like their injured friend owes them some of their money.

Some people can't resist being on television. One need only look to Jerry Springer or reality shows to find proof of this. However, the lottery should warn winners of what they are getting into when they choose to release their names to the public.

You would think that the lottery board would want to push some reforms just to make it look better. If all lottery winners come off looking as bad as Jack, other people will be less likely to want to play the game.

Maybe Jack would have been ruined even if safeguards had been in place. He turned into a first-class jerk.

Yet still, even jerks don't deserve to see their granddaughter die.

That is the worst that could happen.

*Other Lottery Losers*

# Curse of the Lottery

*"I can just see me on a tropical island; riding the surf and drinking coconut wine; chasing the sun through an innocent land; leaving the straight life behind."*

**—Bobby Goldsboro**

The E! Entertainment television network aired a show called "Curse of the Lottery." It featured lottery winners who turned into lottery losers, like Jack Whittaker.

I don't play the lottery and encourage everyone to do the same, but I know many people do it anyway. That reality is reinforced every time I stop in a convenience store. I would like stores with lottery lines and non-lottery lines.

I wonder if I would be the only person in the non-lottery category.

I feel sorry for the people who hang around stores blowing their money on lottery tickets; especially those who play scratch-off games. There is an allure to scratch-off games that totally escapes me.

I can see spending a buck on the chance to win $300 million. I don't understand spending that same buck on a scratch-off game. I have watched a lot of people win a few dollars with scratch-offs and then turn around and buy more until they blow it all.

Scratch-off games are not a form of gambling; they are a form of boredom killing.

Many lottery players are like the man in the Bobby Goldsboro song. They want to escape from where they are. It is the same reason that people do drugs, drink, and have other issues. They are looking for a way out of their current lives.

They hope the lottery will solve their problems. They think things will be better on a tropical island.

If tropical islands were perfect, everyone would live there. Professional beachcombing may not be all it is made out to be.

Unlike the insinuation of the E! Entertainment television show, winning the lottery is not like the curse of King Tut's tomb. The problem is that people do not handle the change in lifestyle well.

Many lottery players are people who already have issues. They want to be rid of problems and hope that the lottery is the answer. Although it doesn't happen often, one of those unhappy people sometimes win.

Once they win, they expect their problems to be gone. They won't be. Money will cause those problems to multiply.

Most people have boundaries, and money is one of the biggest. People don't take fifty of their closest "friends" to Las Vegas because they can't afford to.

Lottery winners can suddenly afford to do stupid things, and they do so until the money runs out. The friends go at about the same time the money does.

Jack Whittaker is a classic example of where money met bad habits. Blowing thousands in strip clubs, indulging his granddaughter, and his generally obnoxious behavior could not have happened without unlimited money.

It was not a curse. It was a guy with no control. The money did not create Jack's bad habits; it let him practice them without boundaries.

If Jack had spent some money on some good psychological help, he might have kept more money and had a better quality of life. It certainly couldn't have hurt. His "strip club and casino therapy" was expensive and did not pay off.

I have heard that 90% of people who win the lottery run through the money in five years. A lot of people are doing things wrong.

They don't look at the winnings as a chance to provide security, give back to the world, or take care of their family.

They look at the money as a way to leave the straight life behind.

As long as they see money as a way to fix their other problems, they are never going to have it long.

That is not a curse; it is just the way the world works.

# Virginia Merida: Get Rich or Die Trying

*"Get Rich or Die Trying"*

**—50 Cent**

When Lottery winner Virginia Merida died in Newport, Ky., it was days before anyone found her. Five years after hitting a big jackpot, she died by herself at age 51.

A large lump sum overwhelms most people. They make mistakes and let people take advantage of them.

Some people use the example of lottery winner's wasted lives to say that money is bad.

Money isn't evil. Even quick money is not evil. Money allows us to feed our families and to live a high quality life. It is the exchange system we use to translate work product into rewards.

Get rich or die is not a motto to many people, it is a lifestyle. Like sex, drugs or rock and roll, money can become an obsession.

It is said that money is the root of all evil. A television minister named Reverend Ike said the lack of money is the root of all evil.

Lack of respect for money is really the root of all evil.

People that set financial limits and goals live happily. Those that don't are unhappy, lonely, or make fools out of themselves.

The unhappy people did not have respect for the money. Money is like fire or a dangerous substance. You have to understand that it can do both good and harm.

If you go into a strip joint with $545,000 in cash, you don't have respect for the money.

Most people have friends within 15% of their own income class. When someone wealthy has friends who are poor, it is hard for them to do the same things socially.

Some big spenders think that money can buy them love, friends, or happiness.

What kind of person would want "love" from someone who wants them only for their money?

It would be a lot cheaper and productive to dump the "friend" and spend the money on a good therapist.

I have a hard time feeling sorry for people who had a chance to do it right and screwed up. They should have gotten some good advisers and restricted the money in ways that kept themselves under control.

I get angry about those who leech off of injured people. I wish there was a way to put them in jail or bury them under the jail.

There is not a law against being stupid. When a 60-year-old lottery winner suddenly gets an 18-year-old lover, the lover is not with them for their looks.

I really don't understand the inner mind of people who leech.

How much self-respect can someone like that have? I wonder how people get up in the morning, knowing they are going to suck money from someone else.

People who earn money learn to respect its power. You don't see many self-made millionaires doing the stupid things that lottery winners are known for.

Go to a self-made person and see if they are paying people to be their friends; it does not happen. The self-made person has sweat and stress invested in creating that money.

The money has earned its proper respect.

I'm not sure what killed Virginia Merida but her lottery induced lifestyle did not help. She lost respect for her money and for herself.

She managed to be rich and die trying.

# David Edwards: Another Lottery Loser

*"The world's original hard luck story and a hard time losing man."*

**-Jim Croce**

In light of increasing media cost consciousness, news outlets can save money by pre-arranging a "fill in the blanks" news story.

It would say:

Powerball winner _____ is in trouble with the law again. This is the _____ time the jackpot recipient has been arrested.

There are reports that he/she has spent all of their money in _____ years. There have been _____ lawsuits filed against him/her and family members in the past year.

The media should have the story ready. They are going to use it over and over again.

A chance to "fill in the blanks" came from Powerball winner David Edwards, who hails from Ashland, Kentucky.

Ken Hart at the *Ashland Independent* newspaper has written a number of articles about Edwards and his wife Shawna.

Edwards won a $41 million Powerball and took home $27 million in August, 2001. Six years later, the money was apparently gone.

Edwards was evicted from his $1.2 million home in Palm Beach Garden, Florida for not paying his association dues. Shortly thereafter, Edwards was evicted from a storage unit that he was apparently living in. The items in storage were auctioned to pay Edwards' storage fees.

His wife was arrested for not paying $17,000 in back child support. She was released and then arrested again; she missed a court date and failed a drug test.

You would think someone who won the lottery would get it right.

About a week after Edwards won the lottery, I watched him on television and predicted that he would run through all the money. He had every red flag for disaster. An out-of-work ex-con, Edwards immediately acquired an entourage and went on a buying spree. He was all over the media, and I remember him saying that he was going to meet with financial advisors.

If I had been Edwards' financial adviser, I would not put it on my resume.

I'm not sure that even the best adviser could have kept Edwards from running through the money. However, there would have been several options to try. Before Edwards started spending like a drunken sailor, an adviser could have placed some of the money into a trust and some into annuities that would have paid over Edwards' lifetime.

It did not happen, and Edwards became another "shake your head" kind of story.

Receiving a life-changing amount of money is not a curse as long as the receiver takes steps to keep him or herself under control.

Most people have built-in controls on their finances. They work for a paycheck and pay their bills. They have a budget based on a steady amount of money coming in.

When people get "sudden money" from an inheritance, lottery, or other source, they often do not know how to handle it.

It makes them easy prey to family and friends wanting a "loan" and prey to the temptation to spend on unnecessary items.

There is a whole economy built around people who let money run through their fingers.

I have noted a ton of advertisements aimed at "helping" people spend their tax refunds. A tax refund is not manna from heaven. A refund means that the government took more money out of a person's paycheck than needed. People should be saving that money for a rainy day instead of blowing it on a trip to Las Vegas.

If people can't handle a tax refund, imagine what they would do with $27 million.

It is actually easier to handle a large amount of money than to manage a small amount. With large amounts of money, there is a point where all your immediate needs can be met. You can buy a nice house and car and not have any debts. You can go anywhere you want and do what you want.

After that, everything else is just showing off.

It is the showing-off part that gets lottery winners into trouble.

The less flash they have with their money, the less likely they are to be part of a "fill in the blanks" media story.

Edwards is another lottery hard luck story and a hard time losing man.

# The Lost Lottery Ticket

A few years ago, a woman in Cleveland filed a police report claiming that she had lost a $162 million lottery ticket. Although she had had an extensive police record, some people gave her story credence—until the real winner came forward.

The woman tried to divert attempts at justice by saying that she lied in order to help her children as well as unemployed Cleveland police officers.

Her explanation had some holes in it.

Her children did not have special needs or have higher expenses than other children.

I would think that she could get the children some school clothes, McDonalds Happy Meals, and a couple of *Dora the Explorer* videos for less than $162 million.

Since Cleveland policemen have handcuffed her and hauled her away in the past, I am not sure why she wanted to split her winnings with them. It could be that she hoped to get some special treatment the next time she was arrested.

She might have been looking for police protection from the throngs of people who believed her story and started searching her neighborhood in order to find the missing ticket.

Most of my clients are people who have been horribly injured. The money they receive is to compensate for a hell that most of us cannot imagine. They deserve every dime they get.

Even though these people have medical needs, they often attract a host of family, "friends," and strangers who want to "handle" their money. These parasites convince themselves that they deserve the money more than the injured person.

A friend of mine has a picture of himself with a President of the United States. He shows the picture and says that the President has the second toughest job in America. Then he will show you a picture of the mother of a brain-damaged baby, and tell you that the woman is the one who has the toughest job in America.

He is absolutely right.

You might think that only the most evil of people would attempt to take money from a brain-damaged baby, but I see it done on a regular basis.

Just like the woman in Cleveland, these leeches reason that their "management" of the money will contribute to the greater good, and that it doesn't matter how dishonest they have to be to acquire it.

Many innocent people believe these self-serving lies.

Since the woman in Cleveland was quickly discovered, the only people hurt by her lies were those she duped into searching for her "lost" ticket.

When an injured child's money is taken away, it can never be given back.

In short, the world has some people who will take any amount of money they can, from any victim they can target.

When they attempt it, they should have as little luck as the fake lottery winner in Cleveland did.

# Section Three

# Bookmakers and Other Gamblers

# Why is Sports Betting Off the Table?

*"Every gambler knows the secret to surviving is knowing what to throw away and knowing what to keep."*

**—"The Gambler" by Kenny Rogers**.

I regret that we did not have someone sing "The Gambler" at my father's funeral. Dad started working in a bookmaking operation when he was only 15 years old and gambled until the day he died. He was good at what he did.

During my father's era, almost all gambling took place behind closed doors. State lotteries did not exist, and casinos were only found in Las Vegas. The popular forms of gambling were sports betting, horse racing, and card games.

Bookmakers like Dad were small business entrepreneurs. Though they could not advertise or sue non-paying clients, they still made a good living. Gambling allowed my parents to move from an extremely poor neighborhood to a nice one. It put food on our family's table.

Although forty-eight states now allow some form of legalized gambling, only Nevada has legalized sports betting services. In most of America, lotteries, slot machines, and casino games are still the only forms of gambling that are state-sanctioned. As someone who has been around gambling for most of their life, this trend is disturbing to me for a couple of reasons.

Lotteries and slot machines are terrible bets, and only large corporations can own a casino. Talented people can work for a casino, but there is no chance for those people to ever own one.

Instead of starting lotteries and attempting to lure big casinos, states should license small gambling operations like the one my father had.

For a while, sports betting dollars were flowing to online betting parlors based in other countries, but Congress, led by Senator Bill Frist, shut down that big loophole.

I was in favor of shutting down the online betting parlors. Government entities in the United States were not able to tax winnings or regulate them.

Betting parlors, regulated and taxed by individual states, would be successful.

Dad was able to make money in the days before ESPN

and the explosion of televised sports. Millions of people now participate in college basketball office pools, and there are newer sports, like NASCAR, keeping book-makers busy. Thousands of people bet with illegal bookmakers every week, and the states should be taxing that money to provide better schools and services.

Sports gambling is a fair bet. In a football game, one team is going to win and the other will lose. It is not a trillion-to-one bet like the lottery.

Furthermore, I don't like having a state's tax revenues tied to the few big corporations that own casinos. If the corporate executives were to commit stupid or illegal acts, like those who ran Enron did, then the state could be dragged down with them. Licensing a variety of smaller companies would give states a wider tax base.

As noted, forty-eight states already license and regulate some form of gambling. If they expand their regulatory reach to sports betting and allowed it to operate offi-cially, innovators would have more leeway to create opportunities for wealth in their communities.

As a betting man, my proposal is a long shot. No one is pushing sports betting, while the casino and slot ma-chine companies are spending huge amounts of money on lobbyists and political donations. Even though illegal bookmaking is widespread, colleges and professional teams would fight against the legalization of sports betting. Also, there are people who legitimately oppose gambling for moral or religious reasons.

I am opposed to the lottery because it exploits poor people.

The thirty-seven states that have lotteries seem to ignore the fact that lotteries target their poorer citizens. Sports betting and poker rooms are better alternatives because they are fair to both the state and the gambler.

My Dad ran a fair and honest operation where people got paid on time and were cut off before they got too deep in the red. His career caused him to break the law, but he was one of the most honorable men I have ever known.

Dad detested gamblers that preyed on people who could not afford to lose and hated lottery games that targeted poorer people.

Before states rush off to embrace casinos and slot machines, they should allow small businesses to operate sports betting parlors and poker rooms.

As Kenny Rogers said, "The secret to surviving is knowing what to throw away and knowing what to keep."

Sports betting is the ace that states should keep.

# The Comeback of Illegal Bookmaking

*"But I got to ramble, rambling man; oh I got to gamble, gambling man."*

**—The Bob Seger System**

My father was involved in many forms of gambling, and bookmaking was one of them.

Bookmaking was illegal. Dad had a number of cover operations—such as bars, restaurants, pool halls, and grocery stores, which fronted his activities.

He had a dry cleaner with no dry-cleaning equipment. Just a cash register and a garment rack. When someone brought in clothes, dad had to take them to a real dry cleaner.

The dry cleaner was not profitable, but the backroom was.

With the rise of the Internet, backrooms started to fade away. Online bookmaking became a billion-dollar online business. Fidelity and Merrill Lynch became big stockholders in online bookies. They operated offshore but marketed to gamblers in the USA.

Bookmaking is still illegal, but the law became a joke to everyone except Former Senate Majority Leader Bill Frist. He pushed legislation to shut down online bookies.

I have been a frequent critic of Frist—a big stockholder in Hospital Corporation of America. On this issue, Bill and I agree.

Online bookies need to go away. They lure college students and others into trouble. Online bookmakers acted legitimate. They weren't. They violated the law.

Frist used his legislative skill to get the Unlawful Internet Gambling Enforcement Act through the Senate. The new law makes it illegal for Americans and their financial institutions to transfer money to online bookmakers.

Now that Internet gambling is out, where do all those bettors go? Many people enjoy gambling, and online bookmakers introduced new people to the concept.

Backroom bookies will come back.

Frist and I opposed Internet gambling for different reasons. He fought it on moral grounds, and I fought it for economic reasons.

I wanted online bookies stopped because they were unregulated, they took money out of the United States, and they caused people to run up millions of dollars in credit card debt.

Gambling is a dumb financial move, but I don't care if people gamble within their means.

With the new law, bettors' only options will be the corner bookies or Nevada.

Unlike the offshore operations, backroom bookies don't take American Express cards.

Given a choice, I would rather have local bookmakers than offshore operations. Local bookies know their customers and can cut credit off before people get in over their heads. Many local bookmakers are people of integrity like my dad.

Since his operation was illegal, dad's clients couldn't sue. They had to count on his word that they would collect their money.

Frist and others in Congress did not realize that when they shut down the offshore bookmakers, they did not actually stop betting. They just moved it into the backroom again, which begs the question: why not make it legal?

Governments can tax the bookmakers and take a percentage of the winnings. Law-enforcement dollars can be spent on catching murderers and criminals.

It is hard to take a moral high ground against bookmaking when most states have lotteries, casinos, or slot machines. Lotteries and slots are the worst bets imaginable, and the players are usually poor people.

Sports betting is a test of skill. It boosts television ratings. No one in Kentucky is going to watch Montana play Ogden State unless they have a bet on the game.

Bob Seger was right. There are people who have to gamble.

I would rather it be legal instead of operating out of fake dry cleaners.

# Cecil Fielder: The Sins of the Father

*"I know that I have to go away; I have to go."*

**—"Father and Son" by Cat Stevens**

Even though angst between father and son can be traced to the beginning of time, I thought it was strange when baseball star Prince Fielder showed animosity towards his father, Cecil, also a former star.

The book on Cecil was that he was a well-rounded family man.

Then I read published reports which stated that Cecil ran through the $47 million that he made as a baseball player.

According to an article in the *Detroit News*, Cecil lost a ton of money at the casinos and never told his family. Nothing seemed amiss until the foreclosure people showed up. Cecil and his wife then had a bitter divorce.

*Sports Illustrated* said that Cecil allegedly helped himself to $200,000 of his son Prince's signing bonus. Prince was served by a lawsuit process server seeking Cecil during a baseball game.

You can see why Prince is somewhat hostile.

Money woes caused the destruction of the Fielder family, just as it has for many families. Money is a leading cause of divorce. Cecil's hidden gambling spawned a lack of trust.

Although gambling was a huge part of the problem, Cecil also lost money making bad business decisions; that is really sad.

When you have $47 million, you don't need to make ANY business decisions. You just need to hang on to your money. You can invest it conservatively and live the life you want.

The smart thing for Fielder to do would have been to set some financial goals that would have gotten a decent return with little risk.

If Cecil had put the money in treasury bonds paying 5%, the interest would have been over $2.3 million a year.

Some people can live on $2.3 million a year; I probably can.

There was no need for Cecil to take business risks; he did anyway.

Cecil went into businesses like classic cars, real estate, and limousine service.

Most successful business owners start from the ground up and know their industries intimately. Baseball has no correlation to any of the businesses Fielder was in. Umpires don't whisper hot real estate tips in your ear.

Now Cecil has nothing, and his bad decisions helped destroy his family.

Watching the Fielder family feud is painful. Baseball is a sport that worships father-son combinations. If Cecil could have kept it together, he would be a hero to a new generation.

I don't know the whole story. Cecil blames his ex-wife for the family rift and claims she was a wild spender. He might be right, but I would have liked to have seen how the family would have held up if Cecil had stuck his money in the bank.

You used to hear frequent stories of athletes going broke. It doesn't happen as often now. In recent years, specialized firms have started handling players' money, and many have done a good job.

Also, baseball players make more money than they used to. I remember when Pete Rose's goal was to someday make $100,000. Now the bat boy probably makes that.

Few people get the opportunity to make really big money, and professional athletes have short careers.

Businesspeople can go broke and start over, but Cecil is not going to get another chance to hit home runs.

It doesn't sound like Cecil has learned his lesson. He told *Sports Illustrated* that he is going to hit the big time with a broadband network. He and Evander Holyfield are partners. I'd feel better about Cecil's chances if his partner were a broadband wiz instead of a former boxer.

Cecil is swinging for the fences in the business world and hoping for a home run.

In business, like in baseball, there are more strikeouts than home runs. Like playing baseball, business is not as easy as it looks.

I really liked Cecil Fielder as a player and hope he gets his life together. Until he does, I can see why Prince is following Cat Stevens' advice.

Prince knows he has to go away and not make the mistakes his dad made.

# Showing Gamblers the Way

*"I want you, to show me the way."*

**—Peter Frampton**

My late father was a bookie and a professional gambler.

If dad had gone into a different line of work, banking would have been a natural choice. Dad was a master at deciding how much credit bettors could have. He made sure that gamblers did not get in over their heads.

Big casinos have more expertise in credit than my dad, but choose not to use it.

People used to ask me how my dad collected from unwilling bettors. He could not sue them. He could only hope that they would honor their obligations, and they did.

When you see celebrities like Pete Rose or former professional quarterback, Art Schlichter, get into trouble, it is usually because they didn't pay their bookmakers. Rose and Schlichter did not pay their debts, but the bookmakers let them get in over their heads.

Out of control bettors should take responsibility for their actions, but some blame has to be placed on bookmakers who let them bet more than they can pay back.

It all comes back to knowing your customer.

Certain aspects of the world of stocks and bonds remind me of gambling. You can lose more in options trading than you can in a casino.

The Securities & Exchange Commission and stock market regulators developed a "know your customer" rule that brokerage firms must follow. If a stockbroker steers someone needing a safe investment into risky option trades, the securities firm can get zapped.

Casinos need to operate under the same rules with the same liability.

I keep wondering why states do not make a "know your customer" rule mandatory for operating casinos. If "know your customer" is good enough for the wealthy options traders, it should be good enough for the blue-collar casino crowd.

Take the case of Jimmy Vance, a Kentuckian who is suing Caesars Indiana for extending him $75,000 worth of credit while he was drunk and visibly impaired.

An attorney for Caesars Indiana said, "Some drunken gamblers win, and some sober gamblers lose big."

What would happen if we extended the Caesars Indiana logic to all of society? Some people might drive a car better drunk than sober.

If Caesars Indiana were in charge of lawmaking, they would change the driving laws to allow drunks and dope heads to flood the roads.

It would not be hard for casinos to implement a "know your customer rule." They are great marketers and know Americans better than the securities traders do.

Casino owners know who high rollers are and to whom they should give complementary rooms and drinks. They know who causes trouble at their casino and the casino down the street. Since they know all of that, they ought to also know when to cut a bettor off.

Casinos do know whom to cut off, but they just don't want to do it.

Getting people to play responsibly is actually a good long-term move for companies like Caesars.

Dad urged one of his clients to attend Gamblers Anonymous (GA). This suggestion, coming from his bookmaker, was enough to spur the man to go and clean up his life.

I wonder how many casinos are referring gamblers to GA. I will bet that if a casino sends a gambler to GA, the gambler is completely tapped out first.

Society is suffering because of out-of-control gamblers. Gambling is the root of bankruptcies, broken marriages, and wrecked lives.

Bookies, like my father, understood that there were times when they had to show their customers the way. Casinos need to learn that same lesson.

# Section Four

# My Dad and Some of His Friends

# Insights into Joe McNay

# Joe McNay: A Gambler on This Side of the Table

*"It's a lonely, lonely road we're on; this side of paradise."*

**—Bryan Adams**

My late father was a professional gambler. Towards the end of his life, he was active in helping at a soup kitchen in Cincinnati, which was run by the Sisters of Charity.

One day, as dad was dishing out food to homeless people, he was approached by the Sister who ran the program.

"Joe," she said, "What do you do for a living?"

"I'm a gambler," replied my father.

"Joe," she said "This is the first time we have ever had a gambler on this side of the table."

The key to my father's success was that he was always on the house side of the table. He started in bookmaking in the glory days of Covington and Newport. He then moved into organizing junkets for Las Vegas casinos when wide open gambling faded from the Northern Kentucky scene.

He understood that if the house has the odds in its favor long enough, it will always win out. As he often noted, "You never see them tearing down a casino because people beat them out of money."

First with lotteries, and now through video slots and casinos, governments realized that a very easy way to gain revenues is by allowing and sponsoring gambling.

The games that have been legalized, especially the lottery, bring in much of their income from those on "the wrong side of the table."

Some European countries limit access to the casinos to those who prove they have sufficient assets. Various forms of stock and option trading, which can be considered a more elite form of gambling, require that those who invest in those instruments have the net worth to survive a loss.

In my father's era, bookmakers cut off bettors on losing streaks. Las Vegas casinos carefully monitored their customers and cut off their credit when they lose too much.

There have been few, if any, moves by states and modern casinos to monitor the losses of their customers.

Legalized casinos, which have several games of skill and reasonable probability, gear most of their operations to the highly profitable slot machines and video games.

Lotteries have evolved from a form of gaming called "numbers," which was very popular in poor, urban neighborhoods in the past. If you go into a grocery or liquor store in any poor neighborhood today, you will see people who can't afford to lose even a few dollars, standing around playing scratch off lottery games until all of their money is gone.

I rarely gamble. I can't stand to part with my money on something that is such a bad bet.

My few trips to casinos have been bad experiences for the house. I bet very little and I am a terror at the low price buffet. I play high probability games and won't go near a slot machine. I have a certain profit margin in mind and leave the second that I hit it. In short, I am the type of person casinos do not want to attract.

Making gambling illegal was an attempt to protect people from themselves.

It did not stop the tide but pushed it underground. Gambling for rich people, such as options-trading and sophisticated stock market games, have always been allowed.

When I passed the stockbroker's test many years ago, I called my father and asked, "Why is futures trading legal but betting on the Bengals illegal?" There is no logical answer.

States are under a lot of pressure to legalize casinos and slot machines, and just like the lottery, they eventually will.

Casinos understand their customers and some of the greatest marketers in the world have been introducing many new people to their games.

When legislators do expand legal gambling, someone must think about and speak out for the person on "the wrong side of the table."

When I was growing up, my father would go around to the sleeping room hotels and give out bottles of low cost champagne at Christmas. Just like the patrons at the soup kitchen, many of those men were gamblers, and often the bottle was the only gift they got.

Legalized state gambling is not responsible for most of these people being in this position in life, but the state needs to take extreme care that they are not the reason we are keeping them there.

# Be a Father to Your Child

*"Half of the fathers with sons and daughters don't even wanna take 'em; but it's so easy for them to make 'em. It's true, if it weren't for you, then the child wouldn't exist. After a skeeze, there's responsibilities; so don't resist. Be a father to your child."*

**—Ed O.G and Da Bulldogs**

There is a scene in the movie *The Godfather* where Don Corleone says, "A man who is not a father to his children can never be a real man."

If the Godfather was correct, there are a lot of guys who aren't real men.

Millions of men make babies and leave the raising to someone else.

There used to be a stigma against abandoning a child; no more. There is no societal backlash against sleaze-ball dads; few people care.

Except, of course, for the children involved, they are out of luck.

The absent-dad problem is worst during the holidays. There are two scenarios: one is that the dad doesn't come around. The child might be better off not spending time with human garbage, but it isolates them from friends who have dads.

The other scenario is where the dad makes an annual appearance on Christmas Day. After not being around all year, the absentee dad wants kudos for dropping off an expensive gift.

The other 364 days he leaves to someone else.

I am an adoptive dad and got into it late. My children are what I am proudest of. I learned from my dad, who was a great dad and a great step-dad. Divorce or distance never stopped him.

Millions of men miss out on that joy. If they show up at all, they expect the child's love for throwing them a few dollars. It doesn't work that way.

Parenthood is a chance to make a difference and leave a legacy.

Too many men are screwing their legacy up. Children should be more important than drinking beer or watching television.

I can't just pick on guys. Some women dump their children too. One of my friends was "Mr. Mom" in addition to being a full-time worker. His son turned out to be an outstanding man, but parenting was a solo effort on the dad's part, just like it is for millions of single mothers.

Law enforcement has done a better job of tracking down "deadbeat dads" and making them pay child support.

Most men pay voluntarily.

It's not about the money; it is about responsibility. All animals are capable of nurturing their young. Humans should be somewhere above the level of dogs and cats.

You know society is screwed up when I quote rappers and Mafia chiefs for their glimpses of morality.

Yet both Ed O.G and the Godfather nail the issue: there must be a societal stigma against guys that abandon their children.

Society lets absentee dads skate. I grew up in an environment where the mores of *The Godfather* were the norm, but it was a world where a man stood up and took responsibility for being a father.

It may have been limited to weekends, but fathers were around and involved.

When my parents divorced, my dad moved just a short distance away. He either saw or talked to us almost every day. When he remarried, he filled a parental role for my stepsister.

Dad never gave himself a pat on the fatherhood back. It was something that came naturally, like breathing. He had no respect for guys who shirked their duties.

That attitude is in short supply.

If people did stand up to absentee dads, it might shame them into doing what they ought to do anyway—being a father to their child.

# Friends of Dad: A Smut Peddler, the Ribs King, and Santa Claus is Coming to Town

# Larry Flynt: Business Vision from a Smut Peddler

If you want to start a business, you can pick up ideas in unusual places.

One of my first exposures to the concept of business vision came from a childhood encounter with Hustler Magazine publisher, Larry Flynt.

One Sunday in the early 1970's, my father received a call to bail Flynt and a friend out of jail in Cincinnati. Flynt had previously lived in Northern Kentucky, where he befriended my dad. My sister and I were at home when the call came, so we rode with Dad to the jail to pick up Flynt.

Dad only had enough cash in those pre-ATM days to bail out one person, so we bailed out Flynt and took him to lunch while we waited for someone to drive from Columbus with money to bail out the friend.

Flynt laid out his business idea for the three of us.

"I'm going to start a blue-collar version of Playboy, called Hustler," said Flynt. "Playboy is too highbrow. I'm going to have a Hustler magazine and Hustler clubs, just like the Playboy clubs."

Flynt did exactly what he said he was going to do.

It is impossible to remember the exact date and time of that lunch, but the event itself will always be impressed in my memory.

As years went by and Flynt became a nationally-known figure, I began to reflect on the business lessons I received at that lunch. The guidelines could be useful for anyone starting a business:

1.) Develop a vision and understand where that vision fits in the marketplace.

Flynt knew exactly where he wanted to take his business and how his vision fit into the marketplace. He understood the competition and where his business model fit in.

2.) Be flexible and able to change direction.

Flynt opened some Hustler clubs, but, like Playboy clubs, they were a fad that faded away. He got out of the clubs and focused on the more profitable magazine. He followed the Playboy business model but was quick to react when part of it was not working for him.

3.) Understand yourself and what you bring to the business.

Most people have moral and ethical reasons to not sell pornography. Flynt has no such reservations. He would do anything to make money. He delights in attracting attention to himself, and his brash personality draws publicity for the type of businesses he promotes.

Most people want to be liked. Flynt does not care about social acceptance. In fact, he seems to like it when people are mad at him. He understood himself at an early age and has used that trait to his business advantage.

4.) Challenge conventional wisdom.

At the time that Flynt began his business, men's magazines like Playboy and Penthouse were aimed at an upscale audience. Flynt challenged that norm.

He has always understood the publicity value of going against the grain. Many entertainers use shock tactics to attract attention. Flynt was a pioneer in that area.

There is a good reason that Flynt is always stirring up trouble in Cincinnati. He knows that the city will fight with him and that that conflict will create more publicity for his ventures worldwide. No one in larger cities like

New York or San Francisco would care if Flynt opened a smut bookstore, so he does not go there. He finds cities where he knows he can stir up trouble and get good press coverage for it.

I haven't seen Flynt since the lunch many years ago, and I don't read his magazine. Although I agree that he has the First Amendment right to speak his mind, I don't always agree with what he is saying.

I must admit, though, that it was fascinating to hear him lay out his vision and then watch him realize it.

He is internationally famous and very wealthy. In terms of reaching the goals that he has set for himself, he has been successful.

When it comes to starting or running a business, people need to learn lessons wherever they can; even if it comes from a self-described smut peddler.

# The King and the Ribs King

*"You were always on my mind."*

**—Elvis Presley**

Elvis was an overwhelming part of my childhood. My parents liked him, my grandmother liked him, and I liked him. He was a bond that held us together.

My mother loved Elvis from her teenage years. My dad saw him in Vegas. I liked the stuff he did after his 1968 "comeback," and my grandmother loved his gospel music. He was the biggest entertainment force in the 20th Century and could appeal to all generations.

I had two kings in my childhood. Along with Elvis, my father's close friend was "The Ribs King," Ted Gregory. Ted took a small tavern outside of Cincinnati and turned it into a multi-million dollar food empire. His Montgomery Inn restaurants are a dominant force in the

Cincinnati area, and his barbeque sauce is sold around the world.

Ted died a few years ago, but his children carry on the business that he and his wife Mattie started.

Both kings had similar traits that made them successful.

Both Elvis and Ted started off poor and made it big. Ted grew up in a large family in Detroit, and Elvis had humble beginnings in Mississippi. They could connect to common people because they never strayed far from their roots.

Elvis' core audience was the working class—people who came from backgrounds like his. He could connect with other big celebrities and pack Las Vegas showrooms, but his connection to working people kept that audience loyal to the end.

Ted Gregory was a guy who could dine with the classes and feed the masses. Every wealthy and well-known person in Cincinnati made their way to Ted's restaurants, but it was also the place where working-class people went for their special birthday and anniversary dinners.

At a point when the economy turned bad, other restaurants raised their prices. Ted lowered his. He understood that if people could afford to eat at his restaurant, they would stay loyal when times improved. Other places went out of business, but the Montgomery Inn thrived.

Both were master showmen. No one put on a better show than Elvis. From the moment he burst into the public consciousness on The Ed Sullivan Show to the time of his death, Elvis captivated his audiences with not only musical talent, but also his command of the stage.

Ted Gregory knew how to attract media attention and draw celebrities to his restaurants. Bob Hope, Arnold Palmer, and presidents of the United States came to his restaurants to eat his ribs. Like Elvis, Ted had a sense of outrageousness. *The Cincinnati Enquirer* once asked Ted if he had seen any recent movies. Ted responded, "*Deep Throat*...twice."

That sense of showmanship and outrageousness meant packed houses for both kings.

The real bond, however, that connects both Elvis, the rock-and-roll king, and Ted, the ribs king, is their sense of gratitude and giving back. Many modern performers command the headlines by doing things that are stupid and selfish. Elvis was generous to a fault. At his death, he was nearly broke after having sent Cadillac's to random strangers. Elvis understood that he needed to give back to a world that had given him great riches.

Since my father was close to Ted, I witnessed numerous instances where Ted helped people anonymously. He also participated in major Cincinnati charities, such as the Hope House. Ted developed his close friendship with Bob Hope when they served on the board of that charity. Ted told *The Cincinnati Enquirer*, "I'm a giver," and it was an accurate self-assessment.

Both kings were an important part of my growing years. As I get older and think about how to run my businesses, I realize that both kings gave me models and ideals to strive for.

They are always on my mind.

**Author Note:**  *If you go to the Montgomery Inn website, they have several articles about Ted. My favorite is in the Cincinnati Enquirer in 1989. The author, Cliff Radel, captures Ted's personality perfectly. It also has a quote from my dad. I think it was the only time dad was ever quoted in a newspaper. I enjoyed how Radel described dad's occupation.*

**http://www.montgomeryinn.com/innthenews/tedgregoryribsking.html**

# Jeff Ruby: Following His Gut Instincts

*"Listen to your heart; there's nothing else you can do."*

**—Roxette**

It's impossible to forget the first time I met Cincinnati restaurant owner Jeff Ruby.

I was about 12 years old when my father took me to meet him at the Fort Mitchell, Kentucky Holiday Inn, where Jeff was manager. As we pulled up to the hotel, we saw a man furiously running across the parking lot with Ruby chasing behind.

Jeff came in later to dine with us. The man had robbed the front desk, and Ruby had been trying to catch him. Dad asked Jeff if the man had had a gun. When Ruby said yes, Dad asked, "Jeff, what were you going to do if you had caught him?"

It was one of the few times in Jeff's life that he did not have a quick response.

The incident illustrates why Ruby has been successful. Jeff was about 23 years old and had just graduated from Cornell. He didn't own the hotel, and it wasn't his money. He put his life on the line chasing the robber.

There was no questioning Jeff's guts and determination. It was the same inner drive that would spur him a decade later to create some of the Cincinnati area's most successful restaurants.

Jeff and Dad were close, and I heard hundreds of times about how Jeff started his first restaurant, The Precinct. As Dad told it, Jeff was managing some Holiday Inns and had little money. In order to become an entrepreneur, he sold his car for $5,000 and showed the money to bank lenders as proof of savings. He lined up celebrity investors and started a fine dining restaurant on the wrong side of town.

It became the hottest restaurant in Cincinnati. It had first-rate food, and all the big stars went there. His next restaurant, the Waterfront, used the same formula, only in more dramatic fashion. Jeff has several restaurants, and his empire is growing.

I have not seen Jeff since he served as a pallbearer at my father's funeral, but I have followed Jeff's career through the media. It is not hard to do. Jeff made national headlines when he threw O.J. Simpson out of his Louisville restaurant. As Angie Fenton noted in a

*Louisville Courier-Journal* profile, Jeff has been making headlines for many years.

Jeff became a celebrity in his own right and lives the lifestyle to the hilt.

I was reading the *Courier-Journal* story at the same time that I was emailing with a friend.

My friend is at a fork in the road of life. She has the talent to make it big in her profession, but career success could mean sacrificing her family life and other interests.

It is a tough, life-changing decision. If she jumps off the career ladder, it will be tough to get back on. If she stays on her career track, she will miss out on other things.

It is a choice that each individual has to make for themselves. Some people are happy working all the time. Some crave a balanced lifestyle.

Most people want it all, but getting it all is a hard trick to pull off.

Jeff was going to chase his career at all costs. Although he was formerly married (and now divorced) with three children, his first love has always been his career. It is his sole-mindedness that makes Jeff Ruby, Jeff Ruby.

A guy who chases an armed hotel robber across a parking lot has a fierceness of determination that few possess.

Jeff's "in your face" ambition and high lifestyle rub some the wrong way, but he is living life the way he wants to.

As Verbal Kent said in the movie *The Usual Suspects*, a man can't change who he is.

Jeff is a high roller with a fierce work ethic. He is not looking forward to retiring and spending time in his garden. He is someone determined to build an empire.

If you want to compete with him, you need to work as hard as he does. A guy who chases hotel robbers, and who survived a nightclub fire that killed 165 others, is not going to be scared by business competitors.

Jeff is a guy who listens to his heart and instincts; even if that means giving O.J. Simpson a boot out the door.

# Lonely People, Haven Gillespie, and Santa Claus Coming to Town

*"This is for all the lonely people thinking that life has passed them by."*

**—America**

During holiday seasons, it is easy to forget about people who don't have family or close friends.

Several years ago, I lived on a rural road and a divorced man lived nearby. On every holiday, he would lock himself in his house and play loud music all day. He never played music any other time.

He was trying to ignore the holiday season.

We always invited him to our house and he always refused. It was easier for him to ignore the day instead of spending it with people having a good time.

He was my reminder that holidays are not joyous for everyone.

Some people never have a family connection. Every Thanksgiving, Christmas, and Easter, my late father would go to a "sleeping room" hotel in downtown Cincinnati and hand out cheap bottles of champagne.

The men (I never saw any women) were poor and usually drunks. Dad had come from a similar neighborhood and had done well. The men were proud of Dad's success and appreciated that he remembered them.

Dad took my sister and me to glimpse a world quite different from our suburban home.

His gift was often the only one the men received. I'm not sure giving champagne to alcoholics was a great idea but it was something they appreciated.

It always struck me that those poor and lonely men loved the holidays. They would dress up in their nicest clothes and come down in the lobby or hang out on the street.

Dad's gesture meant a lot to men struggling to get through life.

It's easy to forget that there are people who would be thrilled to have a bottle of $3 champagne.

My father also made holiday visits to one of the richest men in Cincinnati. He was also one of the loneliest. He had flunkies, but did not have any friends. He had alienated his children and was a tough guy to get along with.

Dad visited him on a regular basis.

He would bring this man a copy of the Racing Form, and they would discuss the horses. The few minutes of human interaction with my dad made his day. He would occasionally turn off his gruff persona and become sweet and kind.

My father was practically an orphan and it gave him an appreciation for the people society had forgotten, on both sides of the tracks. Lonely people often put on a tough exterior, and it is hard to reach them.

It is definitely worth the effort.

Giving is what holidays are supposed to be about. The giver gets more than the person who receives.

When I was very young, songwriter Haven Gillespie used to frequent my father's bar. Gillespie wrote many famous songs including, "Santa Claus is Coming to Town."

If a child sang "Santa Claus," Mr. Gillespie gave them a silver dollar.

I sang the song every time I saw him. It was a sure money maker, but even at age 6 or 7, I realized that Mr. Gillespie took great joy in giving the silver dollar.

He liked that his song was famous, but he really liked that he had money to share. Giving is what made the holidays for him.

More people die of loneliness than any other disease. Reaching out to someone could make a major difference in their life. It is also a blessing for the giver.

During holidays and all year round, we need to show lonely people that life has not passed them by.

# Section Five

# My Brushes with the
# Rich and Famous

*Al Gore*

# Al Gore and the Tennessee Bird Walk

*"Oh, remember me my darling, when spring is in the air; when bald-headed birds are whispering everywhere; when you see them walking southward in their dirty underwear; it's the Tennessee bird walk."*

**—Jack Blanchard and Misty Morgan**

I have not seen birds walking southward in dirty underwear, but something is definitely wrong with the weather. It gets hot in the winter, cold in the summer, and extreme storms are common.

Experts say that global warming is the cause.

I don't really understand the science behind global warming, but I do understand that things are getting weird and will continue to get weirder.

I helped coordinate Al Gore's 1988 presidential campaign for Kentucky. Two years later, I drove him from Lexington's airport to a function in Paris, Kentucky. As we drove, I told him a story that I thought was funny. He told me about a book that he was writing about the environment.

He didn't laugh at my anecdote, and I didn't understand his thoughts about global warning.

I wish Gore could have laughed at my story. He would have walked into the presidency if he had been a little less uptight.

I wish that I had grasped his warnings about the effects of global warming. I wasn't in a position to stop global warming, but I would have been more interested and engaged.

I also would have made more money. Ceres, a coalition of environmentalists and institutional investors, issued a report on how 100 of the world's top companies will compete in a "carbon constrained world."

There will be business winners and losers because of global warming. CEO's need to put global warming on their agenda; investors and stockholders had better do the same.

I've never been a big environmentalist. Green has been about making money. Now environmentalists and the moneymakers need to get on the same page.

Like it or not, global warming is part of our lives. When I run the air conditioning in January, the furnace in July and see hurricane after hurricane, I don't have to be convinced that something is wrong. Global warming was a tough issue to get excited about in 1990. It's not so tough now.

It went from only being debated in environmental circles to becoming a serious business issue. People in the automotive, energy, travel, and insurance businesses should be thinking about it every day.

I have not seen Gore in a long time, but I am sure that he is still a serious guy, focused on serious issues. He is never going to be a fun-loving, backslapper and wouldn't think that the Tennessee Bird Walk is a funny song.

But when bald-headed birds are whispering everywhere, we might want Al Gore to tell us why it is happening and how to stop it.

# A Drunk Driver Might Have Kept Al Gore from Becoming President

*"It's funny how an insect can cause so much pain."*

*—Elton John's song "Empty Garden", which was a tribute to John Lennon*

Few people know that a drunk driver in Nashville might have kept Al Gore from being President.

Only 34, Alex was an up-and-comer in national politics. Both he and his law school roommate, George Phillips, had major roles in Al Gore's first presidential campaign in 1988. George was the state coordinator of Gore's successful primary campaign in Kentucky, and he was also the person who appointed me as an assistant.

The Gore campaign in 1988 was like a small, close-knit family. Alex and George also became very close to Jonathan Miller, a then Harvard student who later became Kentucky State Treasurer. The chemistry between the people in the campaign was tremendous, and all of us remained friends in the years thereafter.

Alex went on to serve as a top assistant to Johnny Hayes, a political powerhouse, and widely considered to be one of the best political fundraisers in the United States. Alex later became chief of staff to Nashville Congressman Bob Clement.

Alex was devoted to Al Gore and was convinced that he would someday be President. When the word started spreading in 1992 that Gore would be Bill Clinton's choice as his running mate, Alex tracked me down in a hospital room in Cincinnati, where I was visiting my terminally ill father. I never knew how Alex found me in that pre-cell-phone era, but he could not wait to share the news.

When Gore geared up to run for president in 2000, he decided to place Alex in the high ranks of his campaign. Alex was named Campaign Finance Director for the state of Tennessee and during the week that he died, was heading up a major Gore fundraiser. As he left Gore's headquarters, a drunk driver on a suspended license ran a red light and killed him.

Two eulogies were given at Alex's funeral: one by Gore and another by controversial musician Steve Earle. It was a testament to how Alex drew friends from all walks of life.

Both pointed out that Alex was drawn to politics because it created an opportunity to do good for people.

Shortly after the funeral, Alex's mother sent me a long handwritten letter about what a great son he was. He was not just a political operative; he was an all-around good person.

It is not inconceivable that the presidency might have turned on Alex's death. Alex was heading up the fundraising effort in Tennessee, a state that Al Gore lost by a close margin. Before his death, Alex had already collected $1,000,000 for that fundraiser, and had he lived, he would have likely played a major role in Gore's Tennessee campaign. It is not inconceivable to say that with Alex's personality and political skills, he might have made a difference for Gore in Tennessee and thereby gained the crucial electoral votes needed to win the election.

We will never know.

Like the song says, an insect can cause so much pain. Assassins and murderers like Timothy McVeigh, James Earl Ray, and Sirhan Sirhan hurt society by harming people on purpose. However, a loser, like the man who killed Alex, did the same kind of damage with his selfishness and lack of self control.

The man who killed Alex had been arrested over 70 times for alcohol-related violations. He was driving on a suspended license and was going to kill someone if he kept driving long enough. His life was worthless, but he took away the life of someone who could do great good.

The man who killed Alex received the maximum twenty-five-year sentence, and it will be a long time before he ever gets parole. Whenever he does come up in front of a parole board, I want to be there to let the board know that the man did not take just one life; he took something away from all of us.

Punishing his killer will not bring Alex back, but it will ensure that no one else like Alex will suffer at his hands. We have suffered enough already.

# Al Gore and My Stint as a Flunkie

*"And if you give me weed, whites, and wine; and you show me a sign; then I'll be willing to be moving."*

**—George Lowell (Linda Ronstadt)**

Political candidates don't need weed, whites, and wine to get moving, but apparently they need an entourage.

To run for office means you are never lonely. Almost every modern candidate has a "posse" larger than a heavyweight boxer.

Republicans and Democrats disagree on many issues, but seem to be unanimous on one point: none are in favor of dropping their posse.

Most flunkies are a combination of hubris and insecurity. Many are insufferable, self-important, and afraid to leave the candidate's side. Thus, they make it impossible for "real" people (people who don't spend every waking second thinking about politics) to get near those supposedly running to serve them.

It's not good for candidates and not good for the people that they will govern.

As bad as the "posse" gets on the campaign trail, it gets worse when a candidate wins and puts all of the coat holders on the government payroll.

On my list of ways the government wastes money, taxpayer-paid flunkies are at the top.

They don't produce any beneficial services and often take the place of someone who can.

I've been an occasional campaign flunky, and in small doses, it can be fun. In 1988, I helped arrange for Al Gore to practice with the University of Kentucky basketball team. I drove his car, fetched his Diet Cokes, and arranged for him to have gym clothes.

I didn't buy the gym clothes myself. I had my campaign assistant (a flunky to the flunky) do that, but I did hand Al the clothes and made sure they fit; they did.

It was an important job, and I took it seriously; probably too seriously.

Self-importance is a defining characteristic of campaign flunkies. Many view themselves as Latter-Day St. Peters guarding the pearly gates—even if they are a flunky for an assistant water works commissioner.

I don't mind if the coat holders are volunteers and not paid staff. If someone wants to spend their free time buying a candidate underwear, I don't see any harm in it.

I get annoyed, however, when a candidate wastes campaign donations on a large paid staff. I get out-and-out angry when that staff winds up on the government payroll.

I've watched several debates of candidates running for president. No candidate has ever mentioned cutting back on their entourage or perks.

Cutting back on perks used to be a hot topic.

In the 1970's, California Governor Jerry Brown made national news by living in an apartment instead of the California Governor's mansion.

Brown was incredibly popular at the time. His approval rate broke records, and he won every presidential primary that he entered in 1976. He got in late and was up against Jimmy Carter, who also preached austerity. Carter carried his own luggage and stayed at supporters' houses to save money.

Frugality was an issue then. It is forgotten now.

As candidates fly to campaign fundraisers in corporate jets that they borrowed from their "friends," I wonder how many meet an average person in an average day.

Their entourage can ward off encounters with any real people—except for the occasional photo ops with bell-hops in their hotel suites.

I'd like some assurance that public officials pick their advisors because of their capacity to serve the public, not because of their ability fetch Diet Coke.

I'm not sure what kind of person would really want to be a professional coat holder. Anyone willing to do it long term would have a distorted view of the world.

I don't want that distorted view in the West Wing.

I understand that presidents and presidential candi-dates need to have tight security around them. I'm not so sure that people running for governor or city council do.

Having an entourage seems to almost be a pre-requisite for running for office these days.

I'm going to vote for the first person to break the trend.

# The Curse of the Gifted

*"Time, time, time, see what's become of me;*
*while I look around for my possibilities; I was*
*so hard to please."*

**—Simon and Garfunkel**

I have a number of friends with genius-level IQ's. Some are millionaires, and some are convenience store clerks.

You would think a genius would have a free pass on life. Geniuses should be the top persons in whatever endeavors they choose.

Yet being gifted is not an automatic ticket to the top.

There is no question that Al Gore is far brighter than George W. Bush, but look who wound up as President.

If you look at recent presidents, only Clinton and possibly Nixon have genius-level IQ's.

Both Clinton and Nixon came from humble surroundings and used their genius to rise above it. They had ambition and focus to go along with their talents.

Clinton could get easily distracted. He could go off the campaign's primary message to discuss arcane subjects, or be tempted by interns.

His autobiography is the classic example of his inability to focus. The book would have been a masterpiece at 200 pages. At 1,000 pages, it is unreadable.

Distraction is often a curse of the gifted. There are too many things going on in their minds.

My underachieving genius friends all have the same problem: they can't stick to one subject. They jump from job to job.

Watching their lives is like trying to read Bill Clinton's book.

They also have the burden of knowing that they are smart and should be doing something great.

They don't want to be trapped in dead-end jobs and constantly in search of outlets that will allow them to use their great intellects.

Many people do well in menial jobs. One of my happiest friends is a bricklayer. He was in the bottom 15% on the college ACT test.

It took all of his focus to get a college degree. He used that work ethic to build a great business.

He is not longing to be a poet or chemist.

I fall into the situationally-gifted category. I'm like a better-functioning version of Dustin Hoffman's character in *Rain Man*.

I know about sports, but only certain sports. I could manage a major league baseball team, but don't know the basic rules of soccer or tennis.

I can't do anything mechanical at all.

I am a wiz at financial computations, but can't do basic algebra. I can do internal rate of return calculations in my head, but would flunk an introductory calculus class.

I have the report cards to prove it.

Most career choices were closed to me by the time I got out of grade school. Medicine, carpentry, and engineering were not options.

I had to focus on the things that I was good at.

It is that way for most people.

The truly gifted don't have those limitations. They can be artists one day and read medical journals the next. Since it all comes easy, they often get bored.

I don't know how to harness that great potential. A lot of people would like to know.

There are some geniuses, like Bill Gates and Steven Jobs, who put it together and become billionaires; others don't.

Sports coaches always wonder how to get the most out of gifted athletes.

The frustration of watching someone gifted under-achieve is that you keep waiting for the day when they can put it all together and be great. The University of Kentucky had a basketball player in 1983 named James Blackmon.

I saw Blackmon play in high school and thought that he would become one of the greatest players in the history of basketball. I expected Kentucky to win the national championship every year that he played.

For four years, I watched Blackmon at Kentucky and waited for him to develop. It did not happen. Every now and then, he would flash his talent but never consistently.

Blackmon has not played basketball in a long time, but I keep expecting him to walk onto a court and perform like Michael Jordon in his prime.

When someone is truly gifted, you never want to give up on them.

Being gifted is like being extremely rich: no one feels sorry for you, and despite what people think, you don't have an automatic ticket to happiness.

Endless possibilities make the gifted hard to please.

*The Scissors Sisters*

# The Scissor Sisters and Babydaddy's Daddy

*"All the young dudes carry the news."*

**—Mott the Hoople**

The number one musical group in England in 2005 was an American band called Scissor Sisters. They have a platinum album, have previously opened concerts for Elton John, and sell out their individual shows.

Their musical leader and producer is Scott "Babydaddy" Hoffman of Lexington, Kentucky. Scott's parents, Phil and Nancy Hoffman, are dear friends of mine.

I became personally connected to Scott when I was invited to his Bar Mitzvah. Although Scott's thank-you note is worth a lot of money on eBay now, the Bar

Mitzvah was an important point in my life for another reason.

It was the first Bar Mitzvah I was ever invited to. I had managed to make it through my first thirty years without much exposure to religions different from my own. By inviting me to share in a precious ritual of their faith, the Hoffmans broke down a barrier in my life. The Bar Mitzvah marked a turning point: I began making friends from diverse backgrounds.

In a *Lexington Herald-Leader* interview, Scott described his parents as conservative. A young rock star might think that, but I think they are liberal and open-minded.

Phil is a medical doctor. In fact, he is my doctor, and the model for what every doctor should be. He is calm and caring, and he knows his stuff. I have never waited more than thirty seconds in his lobby for an appointment. The medical profession would do well to study Phil and operate like he does.

Nancy has served in many political campaigns as well as on boards of groups committed to social justice. I have attended so many events with Nancy over the years that some have referred to her as the "other woman" in my life. She is devoted to all three of her sons and is very active in their upbringing.

I have left out one tidbit about the Scissor Sisters: three of the men in the group, including Scott, are openly gay. Their music draws on the influence of other gay or bisexual performers such as Elton John, David Bowie, Queen, and the B-52's. Their sexuality is an important part of their act. In fact, one of their best songs, "Take Your Mama Out," is a about a gay man coming out.

I am sure that the Scissor Sisters shock some people, but rock-and-roll has always been about pushing the envelope of social acceptability. Elvis Presley shocked the audiences of my parents' era, just as David Bowie and Alice Cooper did in my teen years.

Phil and Nancy are the perfect parents for a son who is breaking down social barriers. They have spent their lives fighting prejudice and social injustice, and their son is making a social statement with his music.

Each year at his first football practice, Coach Bear Bryant used to have his players call home and thank their parents for raising them. Bryant believed that people don't get to high stations in life without help, as Hillary Clinton said in her famous book *It Takes a Village*.

Scissor Sisters' unique sound was achieved through the talents of Scott and the other group members, but at least in Scott's case, that genius was encouraged by two loving parents. Nancy and Phil could not be more supportive. In fact, Nancy's picture is in the video for "Take Your Mama Out," and Phil regularly monitors the band's message board

"Babydaddy" is very lucky to have the mother and father that he has. They are part of the reason that he has achieved tremendous success.

# Scissor Sisters: Rock and Roll Never Forgets

*"Come back baby; rock and roll never forgets."*

**—Bob Seger**

Bob Seger did not become internationally popular until he was over age 40. He was an exception to the idea that rock and roll comes only from young people.

When I saw Scissor Sisters perform at a dance club, part of me felt out of place, but part of me felt right at home. It had been twenty years since I had been to a club, but the groove came back to me quickly.

I had to wear knee braces and keep my doctor nearby, but I braved the crowd for four hours.

I got to spend quality time with some of the band members while they dined.

It was the first time I had seen Scott Hoffman since he became "Babydaddy," and he scored big points by saying he was a regular Internet reader of my newspaper column. "Ana Matronic," the female lead for the band, was fascinated when I told her that the Scissor Sisters were a hit in Richmond, Kentucky.

I recently went into a grocery store where an elderly woman on a walker looked at me and asked, "How was the Scissor Sisters concert?" I then went to the drugstore where all four people in line, as well as the pharmacist, asked me about the band.

Rock-and-roll bands and long hair touch the spirit of rebellion in many of us. I keep thinking I am hip, but I work with actuaries and insurance company executives. I know those people aren't hip, but I enjoy their company. I spend time doing un-hip things like reading tax law and calculating rates of return, yet I feel a connection to up-and-coming rock bands.

The spirit of rock and roll is always there for me.

I guess Bob Seger had it right: "rock and roll never forgets;"even if you do go to a dance club in knee braces and keep a doctor nearby.

# Take Your Mama Out

*"Take your mama out all night."*

**—Scissor Sisters**

I don't know when Scott "Babydaddy" Hoffman is coming back to Kentucky, but when he does, he is coming back a sex symbol.

The key member of the Scissor Sisters is a media sensation, not only for his music but for his beard.

References to "Babydaddy" and his "sexy" beard are showing up in various publications.

A *New York Times* article said men with beards are the height of fashion. The story included pictures of four famous bearded men: Kris Kristofferson, Daniel Day Lewis, Rogan Gregory, and "Babydaddy."

"Babydaddy" has come a long way. Having known him since his childhood, it is amazing to watch.

Even after producing the biggest selling album in Great Britain, appearing on Saturday Night Live, and becoming a style and sex symbol, Scott seems to handle it well.

If he is in Lexington, I'm sure he will dine with his parents. He mentions them in almost every interview. He is remarkably grounded.

I would become an egomaniac if I were a sex symbol. That is probably why God gave me the body I have. Not only am I am fat and balding, I can't grow a decent beard. When I tried, it looked like I'd been on a three day drunk.

The *New York Times* will not be running pictures of me as a sex symbol, now or anytime in the future.

Scott is the third sex symbol to come out of Scissor Sisters. The lead singer "Jake Spears" has attracted tremendous attention and "Ana Matronic" is held out as a role model for full-figured women.

Although visual presentation is important, it is music that sells CD's and fills the concerts halls. Scissor Sisters have their minds focused in the proper place.

The 2005 Brit awards were a great night for Scissor Sisters as they won three Brit Awards. They beat U2 for best international group and best international album. They are the first non-British group in history to win three Brit Awards.

Scott sent me a short video of the awards. It was fascinating to see the show from beginning to end.

Scissor Sisters are revered in England. They were the opening number for the awards show and did "Take Your Mama Out" with the Muppets to accompany them.

It was also interesting to see how different the bands in England are from their American counterparts.

I'm not the best judge of current music as my taste runs toward "classic rock," but I don't see the same innovation in American music that I saw on the Brit awards.

That does not mean the British have a monopoly on taste. For some reason Snoop Dog is hot in England. I've never liked Snoop and thought he was dead (I always confuse him with Tupac) but glad to know he is hanging out in a different country.

Because of the connection to Scott, AKA "Babydaddy," Scissor Sisters has a tremendous audience in Central Kentucky.

Tom Wolfe's saying that "you can't go home again" does not apply to rock bands. Communities take pride when local musicians make good and will support them in the early and later stages of their career.

I was in college when Exile stopped playing the college bars in Richmond, Kentucky and had the number one hit in the country. It was a big moment for their home city as well as the band.

Hometown pride will also help a band that has long fallen off the charts. One of my favorite groups of the early 1970's, Eric Carmen and the Raspberries, re-united *(this year after)* a 30-year absence. Their concert in their native Cleveland sold out in four minutes.

If their initial visit is any indication, Scissor Sisters are always going to be big in Kentucky. Their concert sold out immediately and gathered widespread publicity.

My message to "Babydaddy" is simple: Come back to Kentucky. Let us enjoy a Scissor Sisters' concert and then take your mama (and father) out.

Even sex symbols should come home now and then.

# Scissor Sisters' Second Act

*"Don't look back; a new day is breaking."*

**—Boston**

*Don't Look Back* was the follow-up to Boston's 1976 debut album. It was disappointing compared to their first masterpiece.

Boston, like many bands, proved that second acts are hard to accomplish.

I've written frequently about how I knew "Babydaddy" of the Scissor Sisters when he was known as Scott Hoffman.

It has been incredible watching "Babydaddy" perform on *Saturday Night Live*, write songs with Elton John, be featured in the *New York Times* as a sex symbol, and help build one of the hottest bands in the world.

It's been as much fun for me as it has been for Scott. I get to write about him and don't travel around in a tour bus.

Like Boston's debut, Scissor Sisters' first effort was a rare masterpiece. It was the best-selling album (showing my age, I still call them albums) in Great Britain and won numerous awards. Success like that puts the pressure on for a great second act.

In any business, coming up with a second idea is often harder than the original. A great debut develops high expectations. A second act has an eager customer base, and people wanting more and more.

It can be hard to live up to.

Some second albums outperform the first. Madonna's *Like a Virgin* was far superior to her first effort. She was able to build on her initial success and craft her music and image.

Madonna planned her career carefully and always took control of her business destiny. The Scissor Sisters have a similar approach. They have spent a lot of time perfecting their second effort and a worldwide tour supporting it.

Scott, aka "Babydaddy", is well-grounded and has a good head on his shoulders. You need both business and musical talent to make it in the rock-and-roll business.

A sad example of a failed second act was Peter Frampton. *Frampton Comes Alive* sold 16-million records and was ranked as the best-selling album of all time when it was released in 1976. We all waited breathlessly for Pete to come up with a second album of its quality.

It did not happen. He was pressured by his label to slap something together quickly, and *I'm in You* was a dismal failure. I feel sorry for people, like me, who own it.

The person I feel the sorriest for is Frampton. *I'm in You* and his appearance in the *Sergeant Pepper's Lonely Hearts Club Band* movie killed a promising career for a talented guy. He moved to Cincinnati and wows the local crowds, but will never make it back to the main spotlight.

The Scissor Sisters will be more like their friend Elton John. Elton's first album was a slow seller, and the second one actually launched his career when "Your Song" became a hit. His follow up album, *Tumbleweed Connection*, was the masterpiece that made him a lasting superstar.

Since Elton is the Sisters' mentor, he gave them a few tips.

As long as the group understands that a new day is dawning and they don't look back, they will continue to be successful.

# The Rich and Famous That Have Touched My Life

# Oral Roberts and Me

*"Now there are some preachers on TV with a suit and a tie and a vest. They want you to send your money to the Lord, but they give you their address."*

**—Hank Williams Jr.**

As an eighth grader in a Catholic school, I was once given an assignment to write a business letter. If the letter got a response, I got an A on the project.

My grandma was a huge fan of televangelist Oral Roberts. I was watching with her when Roberts said he always responded to anyone who wrote him.

I wrote him, got my A, and was on his mailing list for nearly twenty years.

Thus began a thirty-year period of people writing me for money.

I found out that magazines sell your name to affinity groups. In high school, I subscribed to *Rolling Stone Magazine*, which sold my name to every left-wing group in the world.

I was still receiving letters from Brother Oral and many pictures of his prayer tower. I even got return envelopes (Brother Oral never forget to send a donation envelope) with pictures of the prayer tower on the inside flap.

Along with that, I received mail daily from left-wing groups.

I would get letters from groups saving whales, groups saving baby seals, and groups wanting to keep me, the whales, and the seals away from nuclear reactors.

The letters had the same message as Oral Roberts: send us money.

During my senior year in high school, Oral Roberts University made a big effort to recruit me. After five years of being on the mailing list, they felt that I was part of the Oral Roberts family.

I had to be the only long-haired Democrat from a Catholic high school in Kentucky that they ever recruited; I still might be.

It was tempting as no other school wanted me. I was a lousy student with little money, and schools would reject my application within seconds.

Then I started telling people I was an Eskimo.

It happened by accident. I was taking some kind of national test, and there was a voluntary question concerning race. Since it was supposed to be voluntary, I left it blank. That did not suit the proctor, who insisted I check the Caucasian box. I refused, and checked the box for Inuit Americans instead.

My mother swears that she did not have a secret Eskimo lover, but I was angry about being forced to answer a "voluntary" question, so the Inuit designation stayed.

I was flooded with mail from colleges wanting to recruit one of the few Inuit Americans living in Kentucky. Oral Roberts University suddenly had competition.

I wound up at Eastern Kentucky University, which did not care about my grades or lack of Inuit heritage.

Although Oral Roberts eventually stopped writing, others persist in mailing me.

I gave money to Senator John Kerry sometime in the 1990's. He was the friend of a friend who got me to donate. I got to shake Kerry's hand and be on his mailing list.

Not long ago, I received a letter from Senator Kerry. It listed a variety of world problems and then asked for $1,000. He did not say how he was going to solve the problems, but according to the letter, sending him $1,000 would somehow make things better.

Brother Oral was smoother. He wrote me nice letters, sent autographed photos, and never sent less than ten pictures of the prayer tower. I never sent him any money, although I was tempted when he said he was going to die without it. I did root for the school's basketball team if my father had a bet riding on them.

Very few of Oral Roberts' followers voted for John Kerry for president. Some observers might point to their difference in ideology, but I'll bet the real issue is that people receiving mail from Brother Oral are used to higher quality letters.

They had to be thinking that if Kerry sends out garbage when he is asking for $1,000, there could be no telling what kind of stuff he would send out as president.

Thus, Kerry went down to defeat.

Oral Roberts suggested that prayer might be an answer to some of the world's problems. Kerry just listed a bunch of problems with no solutions.

Oral Roberts should have run for president instead. At least he had a plan.

# Frank Haddad: The Man to See

*"Send Lawyers, Guns and Money, Dad get me out of this."*

—Warren Zevon

Many people hate lawyers until they need one. As Thomas Wolfe said in *The Bonfires of the Vanities*, "A liberal is a conservative who has been arrested."

Trial lawyers deal with people who have big problems. There are some people with troubles that lawyers, guns, and money cannot help.

Kentucky's greatest criminal attorney, Frank Haddad Jr., once declined a potential client, saying, "He doesn't need a lawyer; he needs a hacksaw."

There were not many people too hopeless for Frank Haddad. People in serious legal trouble often found their way into Frank's Louisville office.

A biography of Washington trial lawyer Edward Bennett Williams was entitled *The Man to See*. In Kentucky, the man to see was definitely Frank Haddad.

Frank was a friend of mine, but he had thousands of other friends too. His funeral in 1995 was one of the largest in Kentucky's history. He grew up poor, but when he died he was a multi-millionaire who had never forgotten his roots.

Frank was humble but not afraid of anything. He was quick-witted with a magnetic personality.

He had a great sense of who he was. I once called him on a trivial matter telling him that I needed his help. His immediate response was, "Don, you must really be in trouble if you need my help."

He was even liked by the prosecutors he battled in court. His sense of humor helped his clients. A federal prosecutor told me that once when Frank represented a reputed pornographer, he brought boxes of popcorn and candy for the prosecutor to eat as they watched the movies in evidence. The prosecutor admitted that Frank's funny gesture lightened the tension of the plea negotiations.

Frank had a personality that commanded respect. I frequently had lunch with Gary Hillerich, who practiced law with Frank, and occasionally Frank would join us. Once we wanted to go to a popular restaurant and heard there was an hour wait for a table.

Frank picked up the phone and said, "This is Frank Haddad, and I will be there in five minutes." Five minutes later, we walked in and were immediately taken to a table large enough for 8 people.

When my dad would enter a crowded restaurant, one of my father's friends jokingly would yell, "Someone had better get up, Joe's here."

I told dad that when Frank Haddad wanted a table, someone really did have to get up.

Frank was loyal to his friends both rich and poor. He surrounded himself with a number of talented lawyers, including his brother Robert Haddad. They did more free legal work than anyone I have ever met.

It would not be unusual to see a famous politician or millionaire sitting patiently in the law firm's lobby while the firm was doing pro bono work for a janitor or someone from Frank's old neighborhood.

He had the perfect voice to be a lawyer. It was a booming voice that could both command a courtroom and calm a nervous client. People, who call criminal lawyers, or any kind of trial lawyer, are scared and want immediate help. Frank had a voice that gave people confidence in his ability to solve their problems, and he usually could.

If Frank couldn't help them, they probably did need a hacksaw.

The Kentucky Academy of Trial Attorneys (KATA) gives an award for great lifetime achievements. The award is named for Peter Perlman, the only Kentuckian to be named president of the American Trial Lawyers Association.

At the presentation of the first Perlman Award, I was sitting at Frank's table when KATA President Bill Garmer started reading the biography of the man selected as the first honoree.

About halfway through the presentation, Frank realized that Bill was talking about him and began to cry. Frank then got up and accepted the award with the humility, humor, and commanding presence that he always had.

I have always thought that Frank's life story would make a terrific biography. If trial lawyers circulated Frank's compelling life story, it would go a long way in responding to attacks on them.

Frank was a role model that average citizens could admire and other lawyers should emulate.

I have worked with hundreds of lawyers, but none quite like Frank.

He was definitely "the man to see."

# John Edwards and the Wiggles

*"It's a Wiggle World."*

**-The Wiggles**

John Edwards and I have a number of mutual friends. In 2003, I saw John when he was in Lexington, Kentucky.

Edwards met with me for an hour. When he started talking about his young children, I discovered that they were all fans of The Wiggles.

The Wiggles are an Australian children's group with popular videos and a show on the Disney Channel. Not only are they the most popular children's band in Australia, they are the most popular Australian entertainers, period.

The Wiggles remind me of a 21$^{st}$-century, Australian version of The Monkees. They are fun and little children love them.

When we came out of the meeting, curious people were gathered by the door. "What did you and the Senator talk about?" someone asked. "The Wiggles," I answered.

An observer was quite angry that I had not engaged Edwards in a conversation about weighty issues. I said, "He is going to go around the country and meet thousands of people, but he is going to remember me."

I was right.

Edwards came to Lexington several months later and immediately greeted me by name. He informed me that he and his children were still big Wiggles fans.

I can't imagine sitting down with many presidential candidates and striking up a conversation about children's videos. I might have been inclined to discuss weighty issues since they are not big on chit-chat.

I was a state coordinator in Al Gore's 1988 presidential campaign. At one point, I told the former Vice President that he should support legislation to make Elvis' birthday a national holiday. Gore was not the slightest bit amused.

Al did get quite excited when I talked to him about global warming. I didn't know a whole lot about global warming (and he figured that out), but he was more comfortable talking about that than Elvis.

Gore would been a great president, but I suspect that one of the reasons he lost is that voters want a president who can hang out and discuss things like children's videos with them. They want a president to deal with global warming, but they also want one they can relate to.

It's not that Edwards ignores important issues. In fact, he started a poverty center at the University of North Carolina. The economic problems of poor people have been ignored by many sectors of government and the media.

Addressing the plight of the poor is a good way for Edwards to stay in touch with average people.

And if he wants to come to my house and watch The Wiggles, he is welcome at any time.

# Fame, Elvis, and the Millers

*"I can't remember if I cried when I read about his widowed bride; something touched me deep inside; the day the music died."*

**—Don McLean, "American Pie"**

American Pie is about February 3, 1959, the day that Buddy Holly died. It happened ten days before I was born, so it didn't have an emotional impact on me.

The day my music died was on August 16, 1977 when Elvis Presley died. I can tell you exactly where I was and what I was doing when I got the news.

The 29th anniversary of Elvis' death, August 16, 2006 was another breakthrough day.

On a show called America's Got Talent, one of the finalists was the Millers.

The Millers consists of two brothers, Cole and L.D. Miller. L.D. Miller, who is 12 years old, is the most charismatic and talented harmonica player I have ever seen.

He could be the next Elvis.

The Miller's are part of a family band called the Clayton Miller band. They are represented on the college and festival circuit by the Auburn Moon Agency. Their founder and President, Nancy Oeswein, dated me in college.

Auburn Moon Agency represents over thirty-five well-known acts and Nancy often sends me snippets of what they are doing. A couple of years ago, she could not hold back her excitement when she told me about the Clayton Miller Band.

My enthusiasm was somewhat subdued when she said they were a family band, featuring a pre-teen harmonica player. It sounded like the Partridge Family teaming with a teenage Bob Dylan.

Not the case.

The youngest two family members, 21-year-old lead singer Cole and his brother L.D., appeared on the "America's Got Talent" series.

L.D. took total command of the stage. Regis Philben, the host of the show, gushingly compared L.D. to a young Wayne Newton.

The young audience sat in stunned silence. No one had a clue about who Regis was talking about. If they did know who Newton was, they were not keen on having their hero compared to an aging Vegas lounge act.

I knew what Regis meant. Newton was a pre-teen ball of charisma just like L.D. is now.

A better analogy would have been L.D. bursting onto the scene like Elvis. That is why the show airing on the anniversary of Elvis' death was so compelling.

Many years ago, I took Nancy to see the movie *Fame*. It was the story of young people trying to make a mark in the entertainment world just like Elvis did, and the Millers are doing now.

# Alan Stein: The Ted Turner of Kentucky

*"Give us any chance, we'll take it. Give us any rule, we'll break it. We're going to make our dreams come true."*

**—Laverne and Shirley Theme song**

One of my heroes is Ted Turner. As a very young man, Ted took over his family's advertising business after his father's suicide. He became a billionaire and grew his business into a media empire.

Turner fought the establishment and won. He moved into the public eye when he purchased the Atlanta Braves and the Atlanta Hawks. He saw value in sports teams that no one else saw.

The Kentucky version of Ted Turner is Alan Stein, President of the Lexington Legends Minor League Baseball team. Like Turner, Stein had a dream and made it happen.

I met Alan in the early 1980's when he ran his family's bar, 803 South, which was a favorite spot for University of Kentucky students. When Lexington decided to bulldoze his bar to expand a road, Alan went into advertising. About that time, he started speaking about bringing Minor League Baseball to Lexington.

People laughed at him the same way that people laughed at Turner when he started the Cable News Network. Alan tried to get public money to help build a stadium with no luck. Instead Alan got private investors to build a stadium.

Just like Turner, Alan is a great salesman and has a way of getting people excited about his vision.

Alan tried to get me to invest in the baseball team. My family was in the process of buying a house at the time. After an hour with Alan, I almost asked my family to live in a tent so that I could use the money to buy part of the team. I wish I had. The team broke attendance records and is a raging success.

I have never met Ted Turner but he can seem obnoxious on television. Alan is a soft spoken gentleman. Both men have tremendous energy and will go any place, any time to sell their ideas. Turner had a rare illness that was caused by frequent flying in airplanes as he went around the world promoting his business. Alan works by car but is constantly promoting the team.

Most people don't remember that the Atlanta Braves were a laughing stock when Turner purchased them, and he pulled all kinds of crazy stunts to get the team noticed.

Selling minor league baseball to potential fans is a whole lot tougher than selling the Major Leagues. Minor League fans don't have superstars like Hank Aaron. You have to sell the fun experience.

Like Turner, Alan is a genius at getting publicity. He has an opening day tradition of doing something silly if his team loses. He has shaved his head, eaten dog food, and done other things.

My favorite was when he pledged to sleep on the field until the team won. The team had a long losing streak so Alan stayed in a small tent during driving rainstorms.

He developed a less rigorous punishment for the next opening day, but the team lost anyway.

Like Ted Turner, it is fun to watch Alan Stein and his passion for making his dream come true.

# People Who Should Be Famous

# Carl Kremer and the Pursuit of Happiness

*"I'm just sitting here watching the wheels go round and round; I really love to watch them roll; No longer riding on the merry-go-round; I just had to let it go."*

—John Lennon

During the same week that Tubby Smith left Kentucky to coach basketball at Minnesota, Carl Kremer coached Cincinnati's Moeller High School to its third Ohio State basketball championship in five years.

Tubby made $2 million dollars a year. Carl makes less.

Tubby has never seemed like a happy guy. Carl is one of the happiest people I know.

In business, or in life, there are people who don't let fame and money overshadow their core values. Carl is one of them.

Carl and I became close friends as students at Eastern Kentucky University. I thought his future was in politics. He ran my campaign for Student Body President, and a year later, I ran his. I lost; he got 90% of the vote.

A guy who can get 9 out of 10 people to agree on anything ought to be president of the United States, but Carl had different ideas. He wanted to teach high school history and coach. He wanted to raise a close-knit family like the one he grew up in. His goals never wavered.

Carl married his college sweetheart, but the road towards his life's vision was bumpy. His son was born with a serious heart defect and was given little chance of survival. After several heart operations in Philadelphia, he made it.

Carl went to coach at Cincinnati Moeller, one of the top high school sports programs in the United States. Professional athletics are littered with Carl's former students, like Ken Griffey Jr.

In 1992, the Moeller head basketball coach resigned mid-season, and Carl took over the team. He immediately turned them into a national powerhouse.

Carl received numerous offers to climb the coaching ladder. Many big-time college programs offered him positions, and it was obvious that Carl had what it took to coach a major program.

We spoke every time he got an offer, but in the end, Carl always said no. The personal sacrifice was not worth fame and glory.

I really didn't understand. I'm a guy who will go as far as my talent will let me. I couldn't see how my friend could turn down the big time.

Yet after watching Tubby, I am starting to comprehend.

Tubby left a tremendous coaching situation at the University of Georgia to come to Kentucky. He had good teams and could have stayed there for the rest of his career. Instead, he jumped into the Kentucky pressure cooker.

Tubby's personality reminds me of Carl's. Neither of them is flashy and both have strong values. Their teams win, and their players rarely wind up in jail. I can see how Carl could have wound up in Tubby's position.

Tubby may have been rich and famous, but he wasn't enjoying life; Carl is.

Carl is so upbeat that it is impossible for him to be negative. I recently wrote the following letter:

> *Carl,*
>
> *You keep downplaying your victories and act like your opponents are not the cupcakes they are.*
>
> *If your players want to be in the NBA someday, they need to act like it. They need to trash talk*

*opponents, run up the score, and pile up a few felony convictions. Get with the 21st century!*

*Covington attorney Phil Taliaferro has bailed several Cincinnati Bengals out of jail. If you encourage your players to follow the lead of these PROFESSIONAL ROLE MODELS, Phil might give your team a discount rate.*

*Your friend (despite the fact that you are embarrassing me),*

*Don*

Carl ignored me—just like he ignored my advice to coach college ball.

The ability to match your values and goals with your career is a skill that few in the business world have. People ought to look at the model Carl Kremer offers.

Tubby's move to Minnesota is a step out of the pressure cooker. He is no longer riding on the merry-go-round that is part of coaching a premier sports team.

He just had to let it go.

# Ollie McNay: Climbing a Mountain of Dreams

*"Help me build a mountain from a little pot of clay, hey, hey, hey."*

—**Tom Jones**

My grandma was a single mom with a son and daughter and spent thirty-four years loading boxes at a potato chip factory.

My mother was a single mom with a son and daughter and by her mid-thirties was loading boxes at the same potato chip factory.

When guys talked about their fathers being tough Teamsters, I told them that my mother and grandmother were also tough as they were Teamsters too. The rumor was that Jimmy Hoffa personally organized the potato chip factory.

Mom had to have some Teamster-style toughness to break out of the family's economic cycle.

She did not seem fit to take the movie role of Hoffa away from Jack Nicholson. A better part would be Hoffa's party-loving friend.

When mom died, both the *Cincinnati Post* and *Cincinnati Enquirer* did great stories, but the headline for the *Enquirer* described her perfectly.

It said "Fun-Loving Ollie McNay Loaded Chips to be a Nurse."

Mom was a single mother with two children in her mid-thirties, when she decided she wanted to be a nurse and she did it.

It wasn't until I was older that I realized what an incredible feat that was.

No financial aide, no student loans. No mentors, no role models.

She found a profession she loved. From the day she started, until twenty-seven years later when a work-related injury ended her career, she never wanted to do anything else.

Her car always looked like a billboard for various nursing related causes.

What inspired her? What motivated her? She never said. There weren't any career counselors coming to potato chip factories and recruiting potential nurses. It is something that came from within.

She had a desire to make a better life for her and her children. It wasn't something she talked about; she just did it.

I never thought of my mom and her childhood friends as role models, but they were.

I realized at mom's funeral that all of her friends started life in the poorest section of town. None of them are there now. Just like my mom, they struggled up the economic ladder.

Many of their children made a higher climb, just as I did.

The trick is not to be a Donald Trump who jumped from being a millionaire to a (self-proclaimed) billionaire. The trick was being Donald Trump's parents who jumped from poverty to being millionaires.

Mom did not jump to millionaire status but she grew up in a housing project and died in one of the most affluent cities in Kentucky. That was a big move.

Parents are best when they are role models and not preachers. Mom was a little wild and crazy. In fact, she was a lot wild and crazy. The lessons we learned about challenging conventional norms could be lost behind the story of her climbing on stage and tackling Tom Jones.

Almost everyone thinks their mother was special, and everyone is probably right. I miss mine.

As her neighbors can attest, mom was never quiet about anything, but following her dream was something she did without publicity or fanfare.

As her idol Tom Jones said, she was able to make a mountain from a little pot of clay.

Hey, Hey, Hey.

# Mike Reid and Rachel Marley: Walking on Faith

*"Walk on faith;*
*Trust in love;*
*Just keep on putting one foot down in front the other."*

**—Mike Reid**

Mike Reid is one of my heroes. In the 1970's, Reid was an all-pro defensive tackle for the Cincinnati Bengals when, at the height of his career, he quit to become a musician.

He was my favorite player on my favorite team, but he had a vision of life outside of sports. Music was his calling, and he had faith that he would be successful.

Reid made it big as a songwriter and performer. He is a Grammy Award winner who wrote huge hits for people like Ronnie Milsap and Bonnie Raitt. Songs like "I Can't Make You Love Me, If You Don't" show an emotional depth and intellect that goes beyond a football player stereotype.

"Walk on Faith" was Reid's biggest solo hit. It came from his heart. Mike Reid kept persevering until he got to the top.

Reid is a well-rounded, well-mannered individual.

You never saw him mouth off or feel the need to hide his cell phone in a goal post.

If you have a son, you hope he will grow up to be like Mike Reid.

If you have a daughter, you want her to have an outlook on life like Rachel Marley.

Unlike Mike Reid, Rachel has not walked into a stadium to play professional football. She cannot walk at all.

In 1999, 16-year-old Rachel and her family were involved in a serious car accident in Kentucky as they drove from their home in Indiana to celebrate Christmas in Florida. Her 12-year-old sister was killed, and she herself sustained a spinal cord injury. She will be in a wheelchair the rest of her life.

Rachel's life changed from that of an active, straight-A, high school student to that of someone coping with devastating loss.

You can read Rachel's story on her web site, www.RecallingHope.org. Every person whom I have referred to that site has come away inspired and impressed; it is impossible not to.

Little things become big things when you are in a wheelchair. Crossing the street or getting into a building can be a big ordeal.

After her injury, Rachel focused on how she could live a normal life, go to college, get married, and do the things that many people do.

Rachel has done ordinary things but in an extraordinary manner.

She went to college. She was a good enough student to be named to *Who's Who among American College and University Students.*

She got married, had a child, and went to China to do mission work.

Not many people in or out of a wheelchair have the courage to live in a foreign country, but Rachel has a special bond with the Chinese people that she formed during previous missions.

Rachel does not just talk about her faith; she lives it. She is an incredible missionary as her positive outlook on life is contagious.

From the first sound of her voice, you know she is a woman with extraordinary cheerfulness and love. It would be impossible not to hear what she has to say.

Rachel has had a lot thrown at her in her young life. Not only has she endured her sister's death and her own injury, she has also dealt with the passing of her mother, who lost a long battle with cancer. It would depress most people, but Rachel has the outlook and attitude to keep moving forward.

None of my problems have ever compared to what Rachel has gone through. She is half my age but a perfect role model.

When people are looking for heroes, they should forget about celebrities. A true real-life hero is Rachel Marley.

She may not be able to physically walk, but she definitely walks on faith.

# My Family, My Country, and AmeriCorps

*"And I do believe;*
*There's a dream for everyone;*
*This is our country."*

**—John Mellencamp**

When Gary Hart ran for president in 1984, he promoted the idea that young Americans should serve in the military or in a volunteer service like Vista or the Peace Corps.

We have military people putting their lives on the line for our country. However, a greater number have never done any kind of public service or volunteer work.

The charge of President John F. Kennedy, "ask not what your country can do for you; ask what you can do for your country" has fallen on deaf ears.

That needs to get turned around. Public service is not just good for the public; it is good for the people performing the service.

If you look at what Tom Brokaw called "the greatest generation," those people who experienced World War II, they lived the collective experience of doing something for their country. Almost every American participated or sacrificed to help the war effort.

It was a battle of good versus evil, and the United States was on the side of good.

That spirit of public service, self-sacrifice, and teamwork drove other decisions throughout their lives.

That spirit of volunteerism inspired World War II war hero, President Kennedy, to create the Peace Corps. Bill Clinton was inspired by President Kennedy's vision of public service and created AmeriCorps.

My daughter, Gena Lewis, and son-in-law, Clay Bigler, did two years of AmeriCorps service. It was a life-changing experience for both.

They spent one year in Kentucky helping poor people and a second year in Northern Vermont. Gena helped to run a spouse and sexual abuse shelter, and Clay designed and implemented a computer network for a rural public school system.

In one year, they made a huge impact on the small town they lived in. It made a bigger impact on how Gena and Clay looked at life.

Both are now high-ranking executives in the financial services industry. The skill sets they acquired advanced them in their private sector careers.

Both value the concept of giving back to society just as the people of the "greatest generation" did.

Years from now, I am sure that the veterans of the war in Iraq will be more active in public service than those who did not serve. Once a person has committed to helping their country, it is hard to get them to stop.

I think Gary Hart went too far in advocating mandatory public service. I don't want to force someone to join the Army or be part of a volunteer service. The programs and incentives need to be there so that people do it on their own.

There also needs to be a mindset of public service instilled in young people. My father used to recite the phrase from Kennedy's inaugural speech often. Many of us who grew up in the shadow of Kennedy's legacy felt that affinity towards volunteerism.

We live in a world where volunteerism seems passé. Technology and societal changes mean that we are disconnected from our neighbors. Programs like Ameri-Corps let young people know that it is a privilege to grow up in the United States of America, and that they should be expected to pay for the privilege.

They'll find that in paying back their debt, they will grow and be the overall benefactors.

Like John Mellencamp said, "I, too, believe there is a dream for everyone."

Programs like Americorps help young people recognize that the dream starts by helping others.

# History Teachers Who Don't Know History

*"Don't know much about history."*

**—Sam Cooke**

About twenty years ago, I was asked to speak to a college business class. During my lecture, I told the class they should stop studying business and start studying history and English instead.

I was never invited back.

In business, one must understand where their market has been and where it is going. Through the exploration of history, a person can analyze these trends.

I have a passion for history; a fire that was lit by tremendous high school history teachers and college professors.

Chester Finn Jr., my former professor at Vanderbilt, and an education guru, noted that only 31% of middle school history teachers and 41% of high school history teachers actually majored in history.

Several fields may be necessary for middle school teachers, but I am horrified at the poor percentage of high school history teachers with degrees in history.

However, I do not blame the teachers, but rather the administration who hires them.

During college I continually met students who despised history. For me, hating history was like hating pizza or the American flag. It was hard to imagine someone who could not love history.

When I asked why, I learned that many had high school teachers with no background or interest in history. The "teachers" made their students memorize dates and random facts instead of teaching students history.

Students subjected to classes like these should be able to sue the school for malpractice and have the school administrators arrested for torture.

History is about great people, events, and movements in life.

My two high school teachers, Tim Banker and Joe Hackett, could not have been more different. In comparison, Hackett and Banker were like salt and vinegar.

On the surface they did not sound like a good combination; however their taste for knowledge had me striving to become a better student and a fan of history.

Banker, an Irishman who was left handed and funny, coached football and track. During my junior year, I became Banker's favorite student because I too was Irish, left handed, funny, and played football and ran track. Yet surprisingly, I was not a likely candidate for being the teacher's pet.

Entering my junior year of high school, I ranked 110 out of a class of 128. I played sports, but did not have natural athletic ability. My friends were comprised of the top five students in the class and the worst five students in the class. The police were on a first name basis with the bottom five and quickly learned my name too.

Banker helped me become excited about history and school in general, and in the process, I became a good student and drifted away from the negative crowd.

On top of knowing his history, Banker was a great entertainer. Banker believed learning should be fun and his teaching methods never led to a dull class.

However, there was nothing fun about my other mentor, Joe Hackett. I have never known a tougher disciplinarian than him.

Hackett had been a meat cutter in Covington and did not graduate from college until he was nearly 50.

Hackett coached state-champion-winning baseball teams, and I suspect his talents as a baseball coach kept him from getting fired. Hackett, a registered socialist and teacher in a conservative Catholic school, challenged and intimidated all of his students, despite their social class and parents' connections.

Hackett stressed that the powerful must be challenged or they will trample over the rights of the less powerful. I never left his class being afraid to challenge authority; I was only afraid of him.

I was privileged to be the first person to receive an award named in his honor. Hackett and I stayed in touch for the rest of his life, but he was not my buddy; he was my teacher and mentor.

Every adolescent and young adult should have teachers like Banker and Hackett—teachers with passion who actually study and believe in what they are teaching, instead of teachers who are scrambling to stay one chapter ahead of their students.

The song, "Don't Know Much about History" should be seen as entertainment rather than the theme song for the quality of history teachers.

If I were in charge of education, administrators who hired history teachers who didn't know history would only have to remember one date—their termination date. It would be listed under current events.

# Section Six

# Blood Money

# Blood Money and the Pizza Hut Waitress

*"I don't feel like dancing."*

**—Scissor Sisters (song written by "Babydaddy", "Jake Spears" and Sir Elton John)**

National headlines came out of Aurora, Indiana, when a Pizza Hut waitress received a $10,000 "tip" from one of her regular customers.

Buried in the story was an important fact: "Becky", the woman who left the tip, had just received an injury settlement. Becky's husband and oldest daughter had been killed in an accident.

"Becky" didn't win the money in a lottery. She received it as compensation for a terrible loss.

The media spin has been to pat "Becky" on the back for her generosity. The feel-good story is that the Pizza Hut waitress' life will be better because of the "tip."

The person I worry about is "Becky." Injury settlements are awarded for one reason: to help the loved ones of the people who were killed.

The injury settlement was calculated to take care of Becky and her children. The Pizza Hut waitress was not factored in. No one in the waitress' family died.

The waitress' "tip" did not come from an emotionally stable business person, like Warren Buffet or Bill Gates. It came from someone going through a personal hell.

I don't know anything about "Becky" or her settlement. I don't know how much money she and her children received. I don't know if her lawyers helped her set up structured settlements or if she has good financial advisors.

Giving $10,000 to a semi-stranger is not evidence of sound thinking or long-term financial planning. It shows signs of a hurting person who perceived that her settlement was "blood money."

When people receive a lump sum, they think it will last forever. Look at the history of most lottery winners. People think it is incredible that a guy like Jack Whittaker can run through millions of dollars, yet the same feat has been accomplished many times over.

Jack gave his tips to strippers instead of Pizza Hut waitresses, but the bottom line is the same: both Becky and Jack would have been better off keeping the money for themselves.

Going back to Bill Gates and Warren Buffet, both of them committed to giving away the fortunes that they accumulated through business success.

Instead of giving the money to a waitress with no strings attached, Bill and Warren gave their money to a foundation.

The foundation has goals and objectives. It also has rigid criteria as to who receives the money.

Bill and Warren are smart businessmen. They did not waste money once they earned it, and they are making sure it is not wasted as they give it away.

When my mother and sister died, I set up a college scholarship fund in their names. Both my mother and sister were single parents, and the scholarship's focus is on helping other single parents like them.

The scholarship will be helping someone for years after I am gone. It has professional administrators and investment advisors.

Since we don't know Becky's real name, we won't ever find out the final story. We won't know if the money she received from her settlement will allow her and her children to have a better life. We won't know if somewhere down the road, Becky will have frittered away her family's money and be broke.

We also don't know if the "feel-good" publicity from the $10,000 tip will cause Becky to do the same for another waitress, a gas station attendant, or some other person with a hard luck story.

If I die in an accident, I don't want my family to give their settlement money to a waitress. I want them to spend the money on themselves. I have a suspicion that Becky's deceased husband would feel that way too.

Although many media outlets want us to jump up and cheer for "Becky," I don't feel like dancing.

# The 9/11 Widow and the Wasted Settlement

*"How do I live without you? I want to know. How do I ever, ever survive? Oh how do I live?"*

—Trisha Yearwood

Kathy Trant attracted worldwide attention by quickly spending the $4.7 million she received for the death of her husband who was killed in the September 11, 2001 World Trade Center attack.

I'm not surprised about Trant's story. I have seen the same story played out hundreds of times with larger and even smaller sums of money.

Trant called the money, "blood money." Her spending sprees were a sub-conscious and probably sometimes conscious effort to run through the money.

It is a common feeling amongst widows and widowers.

Some people use drugs and alcohol. They use "blood money."

Many people think that if they get rid of the money their lives will go back to normal.

Often, I see a grief-ridden person influenced by family and friends.

I have had a number of widows and widowers remarry quickly and then turn all financial decisions over to the new spouse. Usually, the new spouse and the money run out at about the same time.

Many years ago, I had a client whose wife was killed in a car accident. He received a $500,000 settlement. I invested his money, but every month, the new wife would come to my office wanting to withdraw more. Each time, she was sporting new jewelry, a mink coat, and other expensive items. I finally went to their house and told them they were going to run out of money.

They moved their money to another broker.

Within six months, she had spent the entire $500,000 and left town.

Putting money in a structured settlement and giving victims a monthly payment is the only real solution I have. I don't know if Kathy Trant was offered a structured settlement, but I doubt that she was.

I started out using structured settlements as a financial planning tool and became a true believer.

It is hard for someone who has gone through hell to think clearly about their money. Someone who has just lost their spouse has no chance.

There is a small window of time before people actually receive money to set things up right. After that, pressures and people get in the way.

I feel sorry for everyone involved. I feel sorry for the widows and widowers. Not only have they lost their spouses, but after they run through the money, they are worse off financially than ever.

I also feel bad about the spouses who died thinking that their families were taken care of. People buy life insurance because they want their loved ones to achieve life goals. They don't pay for life insurance so that someone can take six "friends" to the Super Bowl.

A lot of widow and widowers wake up every day asking "how can I live without you?" I'm not sure how, but they eventually start to cope with their situation.

Kathy Trant has been through hell. If her attorneys, advisors, or friends had insisted that she needed to put her money in a structured settlement or a trust, she would be able to live a comfortable life; now she won't.

She can't get the money back from the six leeches that she took to the Super Bowl. People who prey on grieving widows don't have the money or the conscience to help her. I suspect she subconsciously thinks that getting rid of the money will bring back her husband and her old life.

Her husband is not coming back. She, and others like her, need to answer the question, "How do I live without you," by answering, "With great memories and the money you left to help me through this."

# And When I Die

*"And when I die, and when I'm gone; they'll be one child born in this world to carry on."*

**—Laura Nyro (Blood, Sweat, and Tears)**

Like most people, I recognize that I am going to die someday. Unlike most people, I have a lot of life insurance.

I started my financial planning career with a company that focused on life insurance, and ever since then, I've been a believer.

I have purchased a number of life insurance policies to achieve different goals.

I have a policy that will help endow a law school scholarship named for Peter Perlman at the University of Kentucky. Pete is a former president of the American

Trial Lawyers Association, and he was instrumental in launching my career.

I also have a policy that will pay to a charity and another that will support the scholarship fund named for my mother and sister at Eastern Kentucky University.

Few people think to purchase life insurance policies for their charitable donations, even though the concept has tremendous tax and planning benefits. The concept of buying life insurance unnerves most people.

Life insurance forces people to deal with the idea that death may come and possibly in an untimely fashion. Although I was very good at it, selling life insurance was the hardest thing I ever did.

It was impossible for some people to get their arms around dying. I had a medical professional spend hours explaining how he was sure he was going to live to 90. He died at age 50. I hope someone convinced him to get insurance, but I suspect they never did.

Although I am going to help charities and do other things, the bulk of my insurance is designed to assist my family. Most people buy life insurance with their families in mind.

I don't think that as many think about the next step.

What will the family do with the money?

When you hear that 90% of people who receive a lump sum will blow it in five years, some people conclude that life insurance is futile.

Why give your family a lump sum and have them blow it?

Most insurance policies have options to pay out over time, but few people use them. It limits them to the terms, rates, and restrictions of the insurance company.

Thus, I came up with a simple system. My life insurance is owned by a trust. When I die, the trustee will buy annuities for the beneficiaries. The annuities will pay monthly for the rest of the beneficiaries' lives and increase at 3% a year.

When I die, I want to assure those people will have money for the rest of their lives and that they won't be susceptible to quick-buck artists and outside pressures.

A lot of hasty decisions are made when a family member dies. Many of them are bad. There seems to be an army of vultures waiting to prey on the vulnerable.

As Glenn Frey once said, "The lure of easy money has a very strong appeal."

I don't want my family to be in a position where a "friend" can burn them after my death.

That is why the combination of life insurance, a trust, and lifetime annuities works for me.

I know that when I die and when I am gone, money will be in the hands of my loved ones to help them carry on.

# Too Much Money, Too Soon

*"And here I sit so patiently; waiting to find out what price you have to pay; to get out of going through all these things twice."*

—**Bob Dylan**

I see people make the same mistakes over and over, particularly when handling money for children.

A number of children inherit money or receive money from an injury or other legal settlement. There are plenty of situations when children wind up with a larger net worth than their parents.

The imbalance of wealth can cause family pressures. I've seen children use their wealth to belittle their poorer parents. I've seen many parents succumb to temptation and use their children's money for themselves.

In some cases, I have seen parents steal every dime of their children's money. If no one catches the parents during the childhood, the only options at adulthood are for the children to sue and prosecute their parents.

Not a great way to promote family unity.

Many states have guardianship laws to protect a child's money. These laws work when they are followed and enforced.

A major flaw within most state's guardianship laws is that children are allowed to take control of the money on their 18th birthday and spend it as they wish.

Few 18-year-olds are prepared to handle a large lump sum of money. Laws prevent people from buying alcohol until age 21; however, it is assumed that someone who can't legally buy a beer can be responsible for handling thousands and sometimes millions of dollars.

There are simple financial planning techniques to prevent a child from getting all the money at age 18. I urge parents and guardians to use the techniques, but many do not.

I have seen hundreds of cases where guardians turn money over on a child's 18th birthday. It is like watching a train wreck and not being able to stop it.

Many 18-year-olds feel pressured to spend money on their friends. The child with the lump sum will be the most popular kid in the neighborhood until the money runs out.

Eighteen-year-olds with cash are good clients for people who peddle booze and drugs. There are 18-year-olds who handle money well; however, I have a 25-year history of watching 18-year-olds run through their money at a record clip.

I once met with a parent who could not be convinced to defer their child's lump sum over a series of years. Instead, the money was put in a bank account, and $100,000 was given to the young man on his 18th birthday.

He used the money to develop a cocaine habit, and when that money ran out, he shot a man during an armed robbery. One man is dead, and another is serving a life sentence in prison because an 18-year-old got too much money at once.

I blame the parent for putting such a young person in a disastrous position. Many young people who blow their money look back and wish they had a second chance to do it right.

A person's financial profile is set at age 27. If someone is a spender before age 27, they can still possibly turn it around. If they are a spender after age 27, they will probably be that way for the rest of their lives.

Twenty-seven may not be the magic age of financial fate, but it is a time when many people are starting their careers and starting a family. The decisions that an individual makes at 27 will, for the most part, be more mature than those they made at 18.

The best idea is to ensure that children's money is kept safe until they are old enough to make good decisions and manage it wisely.

# Nothing to Do, No One to See

*"You know that old trees just grow stronger; and old rivers grow wilder every day. Old people just grow lonesome; waiting for someone to say; hello in there, hello."*

**—John Prine**

John Prine's song "Hello in There" is about growing old with nothing to do and no one to see.

A futurist named Dan Sullivan wrote that older people often wish to die because they have either run out of money, become lonely, or have lost their purpose in life.

All of those factors come into play when someone retires. Many people retire without planning for life after retirement.

Corporations have gone from plans that provided income for the rest of the retiree's life, to 401k plans, which give the retiree a lump sum. It has now become the responsibility of the retiree to invest the money; many don't do it well.

Loneliness is a factor that many retirees overlook. Many people's social lives revolve around co-workers. Retirees drift away from a social circle they have had their whole lives.

This loneliness can be increased when someone relocates far away from where they have previously lived, or away from their children, family, and friends.

Loneliness ties into not having a purpose in life. It can be a never-ending spiral as people who feel depressed isolate themselves and become lonelier. A way to keep the cycle from recurring is to make concrete plans ahead of retirement to figure out all of the things to do with the years ahead.

Don't count playing golf as a valid purpose. You will eventually get tired of it, and it does not allow you to contribute to the world. John Prine had another song called "Blow up the TV," and that is valid advice for retirees. It is sad to meet retirees who can rattle off every show on daytime television.

Spending more time with your family is a worthwhile goal. If you neglected them during your working years, however, don't be surprised if your children have developed lives on their own and don't want you around.

There are a variety of non-profit, political, and church-related programs that can give retired people a chance to make an impact and give them a reason to stay enthusiastic about life.

Be devoted to causes throughout life, rather than waiting to find one after retirement. Learning about the cause, becoming active, and making contacts before retirement make the transition simpler.

Retirement is not a time to get ready to die; it is a time to get the best out of living.

# Section Seven

# Things to Teach Your Children

# Keep Children from Being Spoiled Jerks

*"Teach your children well."*

**—Crosby, Stills, and Nash**

I helped a young child who is being raised by a committee. His single mother was killed in an accident. The child received a large sum of money from his mother's death and lives with extended relatives.

A judge decided to appoint a committee to handle his upbringing and named a non-related attorney as administrator. I advise the committee as to how to handle his finances.

The child comes from a lower-income family, and few of his relatives are well-educated.

When it came to the issue of the child's spending money, the first thing that the administrator decided was that the child would have to earn his allowance by working with handicapped children and others less fortunate than himself. He also suggested that the child should be involved in youth groups and receive special tutoring.

The boy is going to have a rough time going through life with no parents, and it will be harder still for him to know that he received a huge amount of money because of his mother's death. Helping children with physical handicaps will give him a sense of self-purpose, and it will also force him to recognize that others in life have adversity and learn to deal with it.

Helping other people might keep the child from being a spoiled, rich jerk.

Money can bring power and security, but it also can bring insecurity. People who are rich never know if someone likes them for who they are or for their money. Many develop the attitude that everyone wants something from them, and they are often right.

I grew up hating private country clubs and considered them to be the pinnacle of snobby elitism. I won't join a private club—although in fairness, no private club has ever asked me to join.

As an adult, I can understand why rich people want to hang out with other rich people. In that environment, everyone is of similar financial status, and the rich can feel more secure.

In the case of the young boy, the committee decided that he should take golf and tennis lessons. His finances are set for him, and he will receive large payments over his lifetime. He will probably have friends who are well-off too. Being a golfer and tennis player will allow him to bond with children who grew up with similar wealth.

If you have children, you want to ensure that they are financially secure. There are some steps to making sure that money does not warp them.

1) Don't let them have it all at once. Most people spend a lifetime gathering significant wealth. Getting too much, too young, does not give a person the proper perspective.

2) Make sure they understand it is not easy to come by. Having them earn money, rather than having it given to them, is a good way for them to find out what other people do to feed themselves. I had a friend that grew up wealthy who once complained that he felt deprived because his neighbor was given a chain of gas stations by his parents, and he was not. He could not relate to the idea that many people his age were hoping to get a job pumping gas or making change at a gas station, instead of owning one. His perspective on life was warped.

3) Make sure they know money can do good things. Too many people with inherited wealth spend it trying to impress other people with inherited wealth. If your children know they can spend it to make other people's lives better, they will be happier in the long run.

4) Don't let them think in terms of a big inheritance. I have seen many young people waste their lives waiting for a rich relative to die and leave them a big lump sum. The relative would do them a bigger favor by spending the money on their education and setting up a trust or other mechanism to make sure that any inheritance does not come in as a lump sum.

5) Be a good role model. If you give money to charity, your children probably will too. If you volunteer to do things in the community, your children will follow your lead.

If you want to teach your children not to be spoiled, rich jerks, don't act like one yourself.

# Extreme Economics in the Classroom

*"You've got to stand for something, or you will fall for anything."*

**—John Mellencamp**

Much of my writing is about people who make bad financial decisions. People who take out payday loans and run up debts on high-interest credit cards; people who play the lottery and gamble too much; people who just don't know how to handle their money.

I'm often asked where people can learn to avoid these mistakes. Dr. Keen Babbage has some answers in his book, *Extreme Economics*.

Dr. Babbage says that personal finance should be a part of the school curriculum.

I've known Dr. Babbage for nearly thirty years, and he knows something about finance. He is frugal and has a good eye for investments. His brother Bob, my former college instructor and longtime friend, was instrumental in my getting into the financial planning business. Keen and I both served as Treasurer for Bob's campaigns during his successful terms as Kentucky State Auditor and Secretary of State.

I know the Babbage boys are good at saving a buck. I suspect they learned it at home. Keen mentions that he learned finances from Keen Johnson, his grandfather, a former Kentucky Governor. Keen Johnson was a "saving, thrifty, and frugal" governor, who instead of buying new office stationery, used the stationery of the previous governor, Happy Chandler.

Johnson drew a line through Governor Chandler's name and wrote in his own.

I am afraid that Governor Johnson's example has been lost.

If you look at the saving rate of Americans, it becomes obvious that the frugal ethics of Governor Johnson's era have not been handed down to the current generation.

We have a society where the haves are getting more, and the have-nots are getting less.

There are whole segments of the business world set up so that the more intelligent and cunning can prey on the less savvy. If you go back to Darwin, there is an argument that the world has always been that way.

Education, however, is the way for the have-nots to protect themselves.

Education is the equalizer in any society. It allows the poor to be on equal footing with the rich. If people are able to make informed decisions, they are less likely to make mistakes.

That is where the concept of "extreme economics" kicks in.

Babbage's book is aimed at teachers and educators, but any parent or student would also benefit from reading it. As Babbage notes in his introduction, the United States is facing a financial disaster "that could become absolute melt down."

Smart money management sounds simple: spend less than you make, and save the rest. I don't think Americans, especially young Americans, get it. Babbage has some ways to help them understand.

My grandmother was a savings fanatic as she grew up during the depression. She never had a credit card or any kind of credit and was able to save money from her meager paycheck as a laborer in a potato chip factory.

Today's young people haven't had to learn hard lessons from a depression, and neither have their parents. Both have the societal pressure to spend on consumer goods.

It wasn't life and death for grandma to have the coolest cell phone or computer. She didn't have either and seemed to do fine.

A family member has been teaching their 7-year-old about money by paying him to do household chores. No work, no Scooby Doo. My parents taught me in a similar fashion, but schools, along with parents, need to join the battle.

When sound fundamentals are taught at a young age, they become habits.

If you don't know the basics, you will blow your money. It doesn't make a difference how much money you have; just ask lottery winners like Jack Whittaker. Like roughly 90% of all lottery winners, he went through all of his money in less than five years.

The spend-for-today mentality has to stop. Schools and society have to address the problem, and Dr. Babbage has concrete ideas, exercises, and plans.

All of America needs to stand up and take notice. Too many Americans are falling for anything.

# Rich Kid Syndrome

*"If you've got the money, honey, I've got the time."*

**—Lefty Frizzell**

The *Wall Street Journal* once did a story on the "rich kid syndrome." It discussed how the children of wealthy people have unique problems and issues.

The biggest concern for rich children is to avoid those people who have a "if you've got the money, I've got the time" attitude.

I deal with a lot of suddenly rich people. They get the money from injury settlements, lotteries, or inheritances.

Too often, they inherit what professional athlete watchers call a "posse." A posse is a group of hangers-on who want the rich person's money for themselves.

The posse is usually made up of people who knew the suddenly wealthy person before they had money.

Rich kids and the suddenly wealthy can develop entourages larger than heavyweight boxers. Both often wind up with the same results: no money and no friends.

Ex-boxers can find employment as casino greeters. Rich kids don't have that going for them.

Wealthy children should be taught that there's a segment of society that hates all rich people.

As Wilt Chamberlain said, "No one ever rooted for Goliath."

Rich kids can make it easy for people to hate them. If they flash their money around, demand special treatment, and lord over the little people, everyone will hate them.

Advice to rich kids: people were already going to resent you even if you acted mature. Being a jerk will guarantee their disdain. They will root for bad things to happen to you, they will just never say it to your face.

Rich children have a dilemma. Many only befriend those of a similar economic class and get isolated from the real world.

While I was in graduate school at Vanderbilt, one of my wealthy classmates wrote an essay that argued that the concept of rich people spending time with the poor was pointless.

He said that once wealthy children join the adult world, they will never encounter any poor people unless those people are working for them or serving them.

He had a cruel but valid point.

Financial studies show that people socialize with those who are within 15% of their income class.

It makes sense when you think about it. If one friend wants to fly to Madrid for dinner, and the other only has money for McDonald's, they're going to wind up at McDonald's, or the rich friend is going to have to pay the other's way.

In recent times, technology has made it easier for people of all classes to befriend others with similar intellect and education.

Still, money is a big factor in deciding who socializes with whom.

My dad was a great role model for how to be a friend to the rich.

He had some money but not great wealth. His closest friends were very wealthy. One bought him a jacket that said "professional guest" on the back. He wore it proudly.

Although dad's friends teased him, he was a great friend for rich people to have. He was not out to take advantage of them. He was not involved in their business dealings, and he was the first to grab the check in a restaurant.

It was a good thing for dad too. He sincerely enjoyed the rich people's company.

My father's wealthy friends opened up their worlds to him. They had traveled everywhere, and exposed him to ideas and cultures that he would have never known about.

They showed him where to buy clothes, what restaurants to choose, and which fork to use.

Many rich kids grow up with their guard up. They need to find true friends who do not want anything from them.

Like my dad, I have friends who are much wealthier than I am. They are often isolated, and I give them a different perspective.

They share their life experiences and stories of their travels and interests. I always pick up the check when we dine.

They've got the money, but all I want is the time.

# The Live for Today Mentality

*"Sha-la-la-la-la-la, live for today; and don't worry about tomorrow, hey, hey, hey."*

**—The Grass Roots**

I saw a fascinating poll by the *Wall Street Journal* and NBC News. They asked the question, "Do you feel confident that life for our children's generation will be better than it has been for us?"

Only 27% of the responders said life for their children would be better.

It is a scary glimpse into the minds of Americans.

I grew up believing that each generation would do better than the previous generation. That puts me in a distinct minority.

If the poll is accurate, it bodes for a harsh future.

If you look at any type of business where people are paid on a commission or measurable basis, the most successful people are the ones with positive attitudes.

The history of anyone who's been successful in business will show the same pattern: people with dreams who work hard to make those dreams a reality.

Many start businesses with the idea that their children and grandchildren will take them over someday.

If people don't believe that their children will be successful, that belief becomes a self-fulfilling prophecy. Parents will be less willing to make sacrifices if they don't see a payoff for future generations. The payoff won't come because the sacrifices weren't made.

There is going to be a politician, or a group of politicians, who campaign on the idea of forgetting about the future and living for today.

If some of them win, it will cause an upheaval in how we approach government.

Government programs are based on giving to future generations. The most obvious example is the education system, but other programs, such as environmental policies, promote the idea of sacrifice so the next generations can benefit.

With roughly two-thirds of voters thinking their children won't have a better life, "lets live for today" might be an effective campaign theme.

There are a number of people who don't have children or don't care about the children they do have. If you add them to those who think long range planning is futile, it is enough to win an election.

It's tough for me to buy into the Dennis Leary song that "life is going to suck when you grow up." On the other hand, I've been on the right side of the economic spectrum and don't have the despair that people who aren't have.

Those who have lost hope need to find it.

The thing that made individuals like Franklin D. Roosevelt and Ronald Reagan successful was the ability to inspire and focus on the future.

I can see why people are nervous. Because of rapid changes and technology, the economic world is in a period of severe upheaval. People cannot bury their heads in the sand and ignore it.

Roosevelt and Reagan faced major economic crisis but kept people focused on the long term.

There is a danger that some leaders will push the "live for today" philosophy, not because it is good policy, but because polling numbers say that it works.

# Section Eight

# Winning Business Lessons

# Business Lessons from the Fake Dry Cleaners

*They'd call us gypsies, tramps, and thieves;*
*But every night all the men would come around;*
*And lay their money down*

**-Cher**

I learned about outsourcing and other business techniques in the 1970's, during my teenage years.

I worked at a dry cleaning business that had no dry cleaning equipment. It had two clothing racks, a counter, and a cash register; nothing else. There was no drive-thru window and no parking lot.

The business was located in the roughest section of Newport, Kentucky, which was one of the most economically depressed cities in America.

My father said that "gypsies, tramps, and thieves" was an accurate description of the neighborhood.

The shop's location did not cater to an upscale clientele. Living conditions were bad and the crime rate was high.

I witnessed armed robberies, streetwalkers, numerous fist fights, and a car jacking. I watched a woman run over her soon-to-be ex-husband with a car.

A house of prostitution operated a few doors away. I never wanted sex bad enough to do business with the women who worked there. They were not the high-quality or high-priced type. One offered me her services in return for a carton of cigarettes. Even though cigarettes were only four dollars a carton, it would have been a bad deal.

Their pimp did not fit the pimp stereotype. He was a pot-bellied, retired steel worker who drove a 15-year-old station wagon which looked like it had been salvaged from a demolition derby. He used an old clothes hanger as his car radio antenna.

He had a second job faking illnesses and going to a host of doctors for pain medicine. He sold the pills to his patrons until an unhappy customer decided to shoot him.

There were other events in this area that ended in tragedy. One of the neighborhood children with real potential decided to play "chicken" with a train; he lost.

I had hoped he would break out of the poverty cycle and go on to greatness. Instead he died at age 16.

There was a diverse mixture of cultures and personalities in that neighborhood. None of them seem concerned about owning neatly pressed, dry-cleaned clothes. They bore no resemblance to the people who lived in the suburb that I lived in.

There was one factor that made the dry cleaners a smart business decision. In its back room there was a book-making operation and an ongoing card game.

The back room had far more traffic than the dry cleaners ever did.

I was the "manager" of the dry cleaning section. Since I was the only employee, there was not a lot to manage. However, the experience at the dry cleaners was a better lesson in business than studying for an MBA.

I learned business techniques that were far ahead of their time:

1) *Outsourcing.* The dry cleaning business was the ultimate outsourcing operation. It seemed that two out of three people a week would wander in actually wanting their clothes dry cleaned. I would take their clothes to a real dry cleaner and have them cleaned. Since we charged a markup for the service, prices were outrageously high and we had few repeat customers.

    We did the marketing and someone else did the work. It is a model that many businesses now follow.

2) *Locating in a business-friendly location.* In Joe Nocera's book, *A Piece of the Action*, he wrote about credit card companies locating in South Dakota because that state looked favorably upon the credit card business at a time when other states were heavily regulating it.

Picking a "business-friendly" climate is a key to business success. That is what large companies shop for: lax regulatory environments and other economic incentives.

Although gambling and bookmaking was against the law, Newport was a favorable business environment for the dry cleaning and gambling operation.

With far more serious crime taking place, enforcing gambling laws was not a high priority for the neighborhood's law enforcement community. The dry cleaners provided a legitimate business cover.

Policemen would occasionally visit the dry cleaners, and on one occasion they went flying out of our building, guns blazing, when an armed robbery was attempted across the street. It was like watching a real life version of Kojak; even though I "witnessed" it hiding under the store's counter.

3) *Long hours, low wages.* I worked in the dry cleaners 72 hours a week during the summer and over 40 a week during the school year. I had no benefits, pension, or paid vacations, and they "forgot" to pay me overtime.

Many businesses use this "long hours, low wages, no benefits model" today.

4) *Keeping operating expenses low.* The dry cleaning business did not have equipment and was located in a low rent district. I was the only employee, and I was paid minimum wage. Although the front part of the business was marginally profitable, low operating expenses made the overall business a success.

Everyone involved in the dry cleaners is now dead. Their lifestyles as "gypsies, tramps, and thieves" cut into any chance they had to live to an old age.

One thing you can say about them is that they were good business men. None of them were well educated, but every night when the men would come around; they had plenty of money to lay down.

# Being a Winner

*"It's a town full of losers; we're pulling out of here to win."*

**—Bruce Springsteen**

President Bush's former political advisor, Karl Rove, is an avid student of American history, and I am a semi-avid student of the same subject.

We both studied the presidential election of 1896. I think that it is a pivotal moment in history since the Democratic Party nominee, William Jennings Bryan, changed the way that presidential campaigns were run.

Rove spent his time studying William McKinley and how he defeated Bryan twice.

It occurred to me that Rove focused on the tactics of the winner, while I focused on the tactics of the loser. That might be why Rove has supported more winning candidates than I have.

I have an affinity for the underdogs and "losers" of life. I am a believer in giving people second chances—sometimes to my own detriment.

I also know that the best way to make a person a winner is to put them in an environment where other people have positive attitudes.

Often, when a person is facing a challenge in an area like sports or business, or even struggling with addiction, it is commonplace to see them turn their lives around when they go from a negative environment to a positive one.

It was a simple lesson in Jack Welch's bestseller, *Winning*.

Welch, the former chairman of General Electric, focuses on a simple but often overlooked point: a positive environment spawns successful people, and a negative environment pushes people down.

It is up to the leader of a group to develop and maintain a positive environment.

My late father often said, "If you tell me who your friends are, I'll tell you who you are."

Dad was a professional gambler and often saw people brought down by the people they befriended.

One of my favorite movies is *Carlito's Way*, which is based on two excellent novels by Edwin Torres. Al

Pacino stars as a man trying to break away from a "town full of losers," which ultimately brings him down.

It is a struggle many people face in business and life. The winner inside them can be brought down by their friends, family, and co-workers.

Welch focused his energies at General Electric on ridding the company of people with bad attitudes.

I've been around businesses where it seemed like the employees were the enemies of the customers. I worked with one insurance company where two of the customer "service" representatives had signs on their desks that read: "poor planning on your part does not constitute an emergency on my part."

It did not say, "I'm here to help you," or "I am here to make life better for our customers;" or "I'm here to make the company more money." It said, "I have a lousy attitude, so don't bother me."

Since their jobs were supposed to be customer service, I am not exactly sure what they actually did. Their negative attitudes brought down any good workers around them. I never understood why the manager kept them.

Jack Welch would have had them out of the building in three seconds.

I have never decided if I like Jack Welch, but I have read everything about him, and he has made a huge impact on modern business. The thing I like about Welch is that he understands how firing people can be difficult and painful, whereas Donald Trump acts like it is macho and fun.

Welch said that firing a person is the by-product of helping a larger group succeed.

Some leaders understand firing for the greater good. It is why you see coaches throw problem athletes off teams, and rehab programs that kick out those who fall off the wagon.

I can't think of four people with less in common than Karl Rove, Bruce Springsteen, Jack Welch, and my dad, but they all understood one thing: if you want to be a winner, you have to hang out with other winners.

# The No-Cell-Phone Section

*"Come on baby...don't fear the Reaper."*

**—Blue Oyster Cult**

My cell phone ringer was programmed to the song *Don't Fear the Reaper* until the day that it went off during a funeral.

It would be impossible to have found a more inappropriate song in a more inappropriate place. If the song *My Ding a Ling* had been the ring tone, it would have been a better choice.

With quick moves that would impress Michael Jordan, I turned off the phone but learned a valuable lesson.

At any kind of important event or meeting, I don't take a cell phone with me.

Tom Friedman's book, *The Lexus and the Olive Tree,* suggested that public places ought to have cell phone sections and non-cell phone sections. Although Friedman was not completely serious, I am. It is a great idea.

There are some people who can't live a minute without their phones. They take calls during meetings and answer phones in the middle of church. Those people need their own sections in restaurants and maybe their own part of town. They are caught up in their own world, and we should not disturb them.

At the other end of the extreme are the people who don't own a cell phone and don't ever want to have one. These people need their own quiet section of the wilderness undisturbed by technology.

Most of us fall in between these two extremes. I think other people's calls are annoying, but mine are important. I think other people's ring tones are irritating, but mine are clever. I think other people should throw their phones in the river, but let me keep mine.

I have a love-hate relationship with my phone. I don't like phones because I am not capable of quick conversation. If I answer, I am on the phone for an hour. I found that abstinence is better than moderation.

I can go days without using a phone at all.

I communicate by rapid fire email. I have not one, but two PDA's, and will answer e-mail quickly. I will answer phone calls by sending the caller an e-mail and go to great lengths not to use a phone.

While my friends are interrupting our lunch by answering their cell phone, I'm listening to them with one ear while I fire out e-mails.

In Tom Friedman's world of cell-phone-preference sections in restaurants and buildings, I don't know what section they would put me in. Both of my PDA's have built-in phones, but they almost never ring.

I went a few days without Internet access and I was like a junkie kicking heroin. I wanted to run up to people and borrow their computers. When you figure that I had no computer for the first half of my life, and no Internet for the first three quarters, the addiction is pretty recent.

Friedman was irritated about going on vacation while surrounded by people on their phones. My problem is one that many business people wrestle with: always being on call. I get calls and e-mails at all times of day and night. People contact me at 7:00 a.m. or midnight; I am never off work.

It is a trap that more and more people face. There is a customer expectation that someone will always answer phones or e-mail.

After a couple of days without the Internet, I noticed that I was calmer and more relaxed. Life went on, and the world survived without my constant interaction. I came back with some well thought out plans for my business.

Businesses might be wise to force employees to create "no-cell-phone" sections of their lives. It will give them time to think instead of react.

Funerals are a "no-cell-phone" area for me. If someone wants to hear *Don't Fear the Reaper*, I won't be the one supplying the music.

# Good Deals with Bad People

*"If his lips are moving, he's lying."*

**—D'Ramirez**

There are some people you do business with, and others you don't. Wayne Rogers had a simple way of ferreting them out.

Rogers, best known as Trapper John on the television show *M*A*S*H*, had a second career as an investment and business guru.

According to Rogers, there are four kinds of business deals: good deals with good people, bad deals with bad people, good deals with bad people, and bad deals with good people.

The first two are simple. Everyone wants good deals with good people, and no one wants bad deals with bad people.

Regarding the other possibilities, Rogers said that good deals with bad people will always fail, and that a bad deal with good people could potentially work out someday.

A bad person will always make a good deal go bad, and a good person might make a bad deal right.

Character is more important than talent, a great deal, or promised riches.

It is surprising how many businesses don't get it. Some sports teams don't get it either.

The Cincinnati Bengals should make annual appearances in the Super Bowl. Instead, they usually watch the playoffs on television. They normally have a talented football team. They also make a lot of lawyers and bail bondsmen rich. Every year, several Bengals do something stupid or criminal. Often they do both.

The team had several players you would never invite over for dinner unless you had armed guards around the house.

Paul Brown, who founded the Bengals, was a believer in hiring well-rounded players. That lesson got lost.

When all-pro defensive tackle Mike Reid quit to become a musician, Brown encouraged him to pursue his dream. I don't know if Brown was alive when Reid started receiving Grammy Awards, but he would have been proud. Brown had character and looked for players who mirrored his values.

Because they live their lives in the public eye, it is easy to spot character, determination, and team spirit in professional athletes. It is a lot harder to spot those traits in businesspeople.

Like everyone in business, I've been burned by bad people that I thought were good; however, I have not been burned chasing around deals with people I don't trust.

Even before Wayne Rogers summed it up, I watched my late father do business as a gambler. In his era, you couldn't sue to enforce a gambling debt. All dad had was a bettor's word; it worked for him.

In a world where trust was everything, a person's reputation became known quickly.

His philosophy was "don't do business with scum balls."

It seems like an easy lesson that some people don't get.

I've had people tell me about deals that are too good to be true. It was because they weren't true. The people peddling them had no history of ever telling the truth. I heard my dad tell a man once, "I judge horses on past performance, and based on your past performance, you are never getting money from me."

It is not that hard to figure out who is good and who is bad. Some people will fool you, but if you do some homework and be realistic in your expectations, you will rarely get burned.

If someone has a history of being a troublemaker, they will be a cancer to those around them. They will bring the good people down to their level.

There is no such thing as a good deal with a bad person.

# Bill Gates: A Business Pirate Looks at 50

*"In your belly you hold the treasures few have ever seen;*
*Most of 'em dreams, most of 'em dreams."*

**—Jimmy Buffett**

When a friend turns a significant age, I give them a copy of Jimmy Buffett's book, *A Pirate Looks at Fifty*.

You would not think that a guy who wrote "Why Don't We Get Drunk and Screw" would be reflective, but Buffett is.

Buffett sums up his life in a 400-word autobiography. It sets the tone for the reflection and dreaming that one does at a milestone age.

When Bill Gates turned 50, many were surprised when he stepped into a lesser role at Microsoft. As a fellow entrepreneur, I was not surprised at all.

Gates has done everything he wanted to do. There is nothing else that another dollar or billion dollars can buy him. He has reached the point where professional managers can take over the company without his guidance.

Now Gates wants to make a lasting mark on society.

If he can live to an old age, we might find that Gates' activism and charitable accomplishments will overwhelm his incredible achievements in business.

Even if Bill were retiring to hang out on the beach, it would be a good idea for him to move away from Microsoft. Gates understood the lesson that many business founders don't learn; the time to get out.

You see over and over again instances where entrepreneurs hang on too long. They have spent their life building a business. Once it is built, they either have nowhere else to go or nothing else to do.

Inevitably, the business starts to suffer and often fails. The same skills that make you a great entrepreneur do not make you a great business manager.

Entrepreneurs often become rich, but few have riches as their primary goal. The best entrepreneurs are people with an idea who feel a need to tell the world about it.

It is more like evangelism than profit making. There is great excitement as the larger world catches on to the ideas and concepts that the entrepreneur develops. Once the business has grown to a certain level, management teams are brought in to develop systems and keep the gains that the business has made.

Gates has always had good managers. Now it is time for him to get out of their way.

Gates and his wife Melinda started their foundation in 2000. Up to that point, Gates had never been a great philanthropist or been active in charitable causes. He was totally focused on building Microsoft.

Starting the foundation opened Bill's eyes to the needs of the world.

The move away from Microsoft had to be easier when Gates realized that the next phase of his life had purpose and opportunity. He is not a guy who wanted to hang around and talk about the good old days. He needed a challenge, and global health is a daunting challenge indeed.

Focusing on his foundation is good for the world. It is also good for Bill Gates.

Gates has gone through a period of reflection and decided to do something beyond creating wealth.

I am sure he would shudder if he heard himself described as a pirate. For him, piracy is associated with people who illegally copy Microsoft products and do not pay the company royalties.

I associate Gates with the more romantic version of pirating that Jimmy Buffett conjures up. I watched

Gates as a contemporary who took on establishment corporations like IBM and won. I admired his swaggering business success. He was David taking on Goliath.

As Wilt Chamberlain aptly noted, "no one ever rooted for Goliath."

Somewhere along the way, Microsoft became Goliath. They are an establishment company like IBM, but that is not bad. Many companies like General Electric and IBM were founded by visionary leaders and will continue to produce fine products for generations to come.

Now we root for the swashbuckling Gates as David, while he takes on the Goliath of fighting the world's problems.

It was a pretty good place for a pirate to be at 50.

# The Unsteady Paycheck

*"It's only half past twelve, but I don't care;*
*It's five o' clock somewhere."*

**—Alan Jackson and Jimmy Buffett**

Five o'clock is important to many people. It is the time that they leave their jobs and stop thinking about work.

Five o'clock has never been a big deal for me. I've been self-employed most of my adult life, and my work does not conform to a time clock.

My father was a gambler and never lived a nine to five life. Thus, I never grew up wanting one.

Many of my clients are self-employed trial attorneys. Along with the bond of working with injured people, we have another common tie: we don't know when we are going to be paid.

The attorneys advance thousands of dollars on case expenses and never know if they can recoup those expenses.

The book and movie *A Civil Action* is a good example of how an attorney can go broke working on an important case.

Many professionals, like real estate agents, and others in the sales industry, have the same kind of up-and-down incomes.

Few people are suited to be their own boss. Most people want a regular work routine. Their lives are based on a 40-hour work week and a steady paycheck.

When people tell me they want to start their own business, I ask them if they can really live without a regular income. I tell them to talk to their families and get their honest answers. I ask them if they could stand to go weeks or months without money coming in and how they would deal with it.

They need to understand they are trading their steady paycheck for an "unsteady paycheck."

Many people want their own businesses for the wrong reasons. Like the character in the song, people decide that they don't like their jobs, and that it would be fun to be self-employed.

They don't realize that self-employment means that it is never five o'clock anywhere.

I've told many professionals that they should not go into business for themselves. They may be good workers with good ideas, but they couldn't handle the stress from not having a guaranteed income.

Never being off work can be hard on families. I had a friend try to be an independent insurance agent. He worked a lot of hours and his wife started calling his office in the evenings. She put their children on the phone and had them say how much they missed him.

He went back to a steady paycheck at a big insurance company. He has less independence, but he is still married.

Some people became self-employed because no large organization would hire them. I did not plan to be self-employed, but I could not find a job out of graduate school other than cleaning up at the Kentucky Horse Park. Once I started my financial business, I realized that I needed the independence of being self-employed more than I needed a steady paycheck.

I have an anti-authority edge that makes it difficult for me to handle corporate rules. I have tried to merge my business into big organizations a couple of times, and it has never worked

I had a brief career at a company that decided to impose a dress code. I immediately started coming to work wearing blue jeans, a tee shirt, and a Cincinnati Reds baseball cap.

I killed the dress code and any hope of my advancement at the same time. I went back to working on my own.

Education and upbringing are important in deciding whether a person can make it as an entrepreneur. I was with Barbourville, Ky. Attorney, Sam Davies, when a woman told him that she was sending her son to military school. "He will learn how to follow the rules," she said. Sam replied, "He would be better off if he found a school where they taught him how not to follow the rules."

Sam, who has never had a partner, is one of the best attorneys in the United States. Many trial lawyers practice by themselves or with a few associates. Most have the same anti-authority attitude that I have.

The attitude that makes them unafraid to take on billion-dollar businesses makes it impossible for them to fit into a big corporation.

They produce an "unsteady paycheck," and they never know when five o'clock rolls around.

Before a person decides on self employment, they need to figure out how important five o' clock is in their lives.

# Are We Ready for a Flat World?

*"And I'll be taking care of business, everyday."*

**—Bachman Turner Overdrive**

Many large companies take care of customer service by setting up call centers in places like India and Costa Rica.

Workers are cheap, and it boosts the company's bottom line.

I wonder if the short-term profits are worth the long-term cost.

The trend is called "outsourcing" and is best described in Tom Freidman's book, *The World is Flat*. Friedman is a Pulitzer-Prize-winning columnist for *The New York Times.*

Friedman argues that over time the world is becoming increasingly interconnected, and that jobs which used to be unique to one country can now be done in a number of places.

I've bought into Tom Friedman mania. I own every book he has written and eagerly read his columns. I have his audio books, and I have my TiVo set to record his documentaries on the Discovery Channel.

Yet lately, I've started to wonder if the world is as flat as Tom thinks it is.

I recently saw a segment from one of Friedman's documentaries where he traveled to India to film customer service employees training to speak with an American dialect.

When they teach those speech lessons, they might want to throw in a few geography classes too. It's not easy for this Kentuckian to do business with Indian service centers.

I purchased a chair online from a well-known office supply store. I had a guy lined up to assemble it, and we waited for the chair to arrive; it never came.

Finally, I called the 800 number for the company. It connected me to a man in India. It took several tries for the man to understand my name (Don McNay must be a tough name to translate), and once he got it, he proceeded to call me Mr. Don.

I've been called a lot of things, but never Mr. Don.

I asked where the chair was. He said it was somewhere in Ken-tuck-kee (he pronounced the name of the state phonetically) and guaranteed that it would be at my house in 10 minutes.

He figured that any place in Ken-tuck-kee would be no more than 10 minutes from any other part of the state.

Since he had no tracking number; did not know what shipping service was delivering the chair; and seemed shaky about where or what a Ken-tuck-kee was, I did not have confidence in the information I was receiving.

I asked if I could talk to a supervisor. He said he didn't have one. I then asked if the company stockholders had named him Chairman of the Board. He hung up.

I then called the company's local store. The store manager spoke perfect English, pronounced my name correctly, and happened to be in Kentucky too. She confirmed that the chair was not here. They had sent it to Richmond, Virginia. Even though it was not her problem (online orders are a different department), the next day, I had a chair.

My company does thousands of dollars in annual business with that company. The local manager did not know that "Mr. Don" was ready to send that business elsewhere. She just knew I had a problem. The self-proclaimed Chairman of the Board in India didn't really care.

To be fair, I'm sure that they pay the manager in Kentucky a lot more than the self-proclaimed Chairman. Yet in this case, it was worth it. I'll keep doing business.

The chair incident was not an isolated event. The further any customer service center is from where I live, the less the likely I am to get actual service.

When a company relocates service centers to places that lack any cultural bond with their clientele, where their representatives won't be able to communicate or understand geographic references, what the company is really saying is that they don't care about customer service. They want to sell their product and hope buyers leave them alone; a bad long-term strategy.

If companies want to keep "taking care of business," they need to remember that it is a lot easier to keep a current customer happy than to find a new one.

Even in a flat world.

# Section Nine

# Financial Rip-offs and Soldiers

# Payday Loans and Soldiers

*"Yeah, some folks inherit star-spangled eyes. Oh, they send you down to war, Lord; and when you ask them how much should we give; Oh, they only answer, more, more, more."*

**—John Fogerty and Creedence Clearwater Revival**

I am tired of watching military people being ripped off.

My personal crusade was to ban the sale of contractual mutual funds to soldiers; Congress finally did.

The mutual funds made it almost impossible for "investors" to make money. The only "winners" are the people who peddle them.

As bad as the contractual mutual funds are for military people, payday loans are worse. A Defense Department report criticized the payday industry, and said that payday loans were costing soldiers from 390% to 780% a year.

Wow!

The Defense Department then proposed a limit of 36% a year on payday loans.

Payday lenders said they couldn't make money charging 36%. Can you think of another business that would whine about a 36% limit?

When I grew up in Northern Kentucky, it was mostly controlled by the Mafia. The mob had a term for 36% interest rates: loan sharking.

In those days, charging 36% would earn you a swim in the Ohio River with a cement overcoat attached.

If a loan shark had charged 390% to 780%, not only would they have wound up in the river, someone would have thrown all their friends and relatives in too.

I'm angry about people continuing to rip off soldiers and military personnel. Thousands of soldiers are deployed to foreign countries, and some come back in body bags.

It is un-American to let big corporations rip them off.

When I wrote about Fidelity Investments selling contractual mutual funds, I suggested that Peter Lynch, Vice Chair of Fidelity, be sent to Iraq in place of a soldier who purchased one of his funds.

In addition to sending Lynch, I want the payday lenders to make the same trip.

Yet as much as I want to blame everything on Lynch and the payday people, you have to wonder why military people can't steer clear of them. The American education system has fallen flat in teaching financial literacy.

Roughly 17% of servicemen and women use payday loans. That is an incredibly high percentage, and military people need to know about better options; like pawnbrokers. Even they are better than payday lenders.

Before we send soldiers off to fight and die, we need to spend a few minutes and teach them how to handle money.

# Defense Department Proposal Did Not Protect Soldiers

***"Don't take me half the way."***

**—Crystal Gayle**

I heard that the Department of Defense was issuing a proposed rule titled, "Limitations on Terms of Consumer Credit Extended to Service Members and Dependants."

My first reaction was jubilation.

I've frequently written about financial companies taking advantage of military personnel. I thought the solution had finally come.

Then I read the proposal. I am not going to hang a sign that reads, "Mission accomplished."

The proposal does some good things. It limits payday lenders, vehicle title lenders, and refund anticipation lenders to "only" 36% interest.

Believe it or not, 36% is a huge improvement. Payday lenders claim they can't make it on such paltry amounts. Steven Schlein, spokesperson for a payday industry trade group, said that after these regulations become effective, "there won't be any payday loans to military people."

We ought to make that day a national holiday.

I would celebrate, but I know it is a wasted effort.

Predatory lenders will be back. Financial service companies have high-powered lawyers and lobbyists that will help them get back in business.

It won't be hard since the Department of Defense proposal is filled with loopholes.

The rules don't apply to rent-to-own companies or banks that charge fees for high-interest credit cards. The combination of fees and interest could easily push a soldier's credit card rate above 36%.

If a government ban does not cover all the loopholes, it is useless. I learned that lesson the hard way.

I've spent almost all of my working life setting up structured settlements. Structured settlements are designed to keep injury victims from running through their money.

In the 1990's, some smart people figured out how to buy the structured settlement payments from injured people and make huge profits. Several of us lobbied state and federal legislatures, pushing for laws that would keep settlement purchasers under control.

Kentucky was the first state with model legislation, and it passed unanimously. Almost every state and eventually the federal government put laws on the books, but all left some loopholes.

We could have made a proposal that completely put the purchasers out of business; we didn't. They decreased activity for a couple of years, but now they have come back stronger than ever.

A bunch of new players entered into purchasing structured settlements, including a corporation that offers structured settlements to injured people. They set up structured settlements and then send the injured people letters asking if they want to sell them back.

The settlement purchasers figured out the loopholes just like the payday lenders will do for military personnel and their families.

Instead of a 14-page proposal on the *Federal Register*, I could amend the Defense Department proposal to three simple points:

1) No financial institution may charge a military person or their families a predatory interest rate or fee.

2) If a financial institution is found guilty of charging a predatory interest rate, the corporation will be immediately dissolved, and the assets (including all personal assets belonging to its officers and directors) shall be forfeited to the U.S. Treasury.

3) If this act occurs during a time of war, the company officers and directors will be conscripted into the armed services and will serve in the war zone for the duration of battle.

I don't think the Department of Defense proposal will keep military personnel from being ripped off.

I know my proposal will.

This is an issue where we need to say mission accomplished.

# Peter Lynch's Fidelity Fined $400,000 for Misleading Troops

*There's gonna be hell, when you hear mother freedom start ringing her bell. It's gonna feel like the whole wide world is raining down on you; brought to you courtesy of the Red, White, and Blue."*

—Toby Keith

In August, 2004, I wrote a newspaper column entitled "Save Our Soldiers from Peter Lynch."

Fidelity was peddling an archaic style of mutual fund to military people called contractual mutual funds.

A contractual mutual fund is a terrible deal. Congress finally outlawed it. If Lynch and Fidelity had truly thought that contractual funds were great, they would have made Lynch's famous Magellan Fund contractual; they did not.

Military people have often been prey for questionable financial operators such as payday lenders. Soldiers are often young and financially inexperienced but still make decent money.

I am willing to bet that Peter Lynch does not have his money in a contractual fund, nor do his Hollywood pals like Lily Tomlin. Fidelity only pushed the stuff on military people.

I asked people to stand up for our soldiers and write to everyone they could about the problem. Many groups that support the military did the same.

Finally, the National Association of Securities Dealers (NASD), a group with real clout, listened.

The NASD reached a settlement with Fidelity Investments Institutional Services. Fidelity agreed to pay $400,000 to settle a complaint accusing them of producing misleading sales materials for the Fidelity Destiny I and Fidelity Destiny II contractual mutual funds.

Fidelity will not admit any wrongdoing, but the sales literature that they gave to soldiers fail to mention the 50% sales charge that soldiers were to pay on the funds.

A pretty big OOPS! The fund doesn't look so good when you take 50% off the top.

Fidelity sold a lot of this product to soldiers through First Command Financial Services, a company which paid $12 million to settle regulatory charges stating it mislead soldiers about the fees and performance of the contractual plans First Command was peddling.

Even though $400,000 is chump change to a guy like Peter Lynch and a billion-dollar company like Fidelity, the settlement is a black mark on their record.

People ask why I single out Mr. Lynch. At the time when contractual funds were being peddled to soldiers, Lynch was using his "Mr. Clean" image to do television commercials for Fidelity with his Hollywood chums Lily Tomlin and Don Rickles.

Lynch and Fidelity can't have it both ways. They can't use the stellar returns that Lynch achieved with his Magellan fund to attract high-end customers while selling garbage to soldiers.

It is like a fundamentalist church with a strip club and casino in the basement.

I'm hoping that the fine cost Lynch and Fidelity a lot more than the $400,000 that they forked over.

Military people do their job with more honor and courage than I will ever have.

It's why I get angry when financial companies take advantage of them.

When Americans find out that Peter Lynch and his Fidelity Company were not playing straight with soldiers, I hope there will be hell. I hope Americans make the leaders at Fidelity feel like the whole world is raining down on them; brought to them courtesy of the red, white, and blue.

# Section Ten

# Credit Cards and Other Sucker Bets

# Credit Card Companies: Sticking It to Poor People

*"So welcome back baby, to the poor side of town."*

**—Johnny Rivers**

Technology has made it easier for some businesses to take advantage of the poor. This is especially true of bank credit cards companies.

I know someone who has a credit card with a $650 credit limit.

This is his only credit card, and he has been paying the minimum payment each month. He has not been late with a payment in over a year.

His credit card statement showed the annual interest rate on the card is 18.90%. This means the bank is making about 16% in interest over what they pay for money deposited in their bank. As though that rate were not high enough, the bank makes it worse by assessing a number of fees.

He ran the card to the limit last Christmas and has been trying to pay it down since then. After several months, he got his debt down to about $600. In May, they charged him an $89 annual "membership" fee to renew his card.

Eighty-nine dollars equals 14% of his credit line. To make matters worse, he was hit with a $28.70 fee (about 4% of his credit line) because the $89 "membership" fee caused him to go over the $650 limit.

Even though he has been a good customer, the company wants to take advantage of him by charging 18% of his total credit line just to keep the card open. They did not increase his credit limit, so he can't use the card to buy things. The card was marketed to people trying to improve their credit history, but now his credit report is damaged because the excessive fee put him over his credit limit.

The fee is too small to get an attorney to help him fight it. He tried writing, but they have outsourced customer service to people who don't respond to letters. He called and talked to a woman who said she would waive his fees if he cancelled his card, but that would have left him with no credit card. When he asked to speak to someone about waiving the fees and keeping the card, she said she was transferring him to another department and then hung up on him.

If he gets mad and refuses to make his credit card payments, it will completely destroy the credit history that he is trying to rebuild.

Now that technology is better, it is easier for computers to pinpoint people who fit the bank's model. Technology has also made it possible for bill collectors to get more aggressive in their collection practices when people are late on payments.

I hear stories of collectors calling long-lost family members and neighbors to put pressure on debtors. It is illegal, but the agencies that regulate banks aren't doing much to help poor people, and the collectors know it. Even when regulators want to help, most poor people don't know the law or who to call.

The card holder is paying at least 18% in fees and then 18.90% in interest on top of that. With the balance increasing at that rate, the debt will never go away, and he will never get a good credit history.

His credit card company will make sure that he never gets away from the poor side of town.

# MBNA Claims to Have Talked to My Dead Mother

*"I'll be coming home, wait for me."*

**—Righteous Brothers, "Unchained Melody,"
(Theme from the movie, "Ghost")**

My mother allegedly died on April 2, 2006. I say allegedly because a collector representing MBNA said he talked to her on June 21, 2006.

Until I saw a letter from Dale Lamb, I felt pretty certain my mother was dead.

I viewed her lifeless body at the hospital. A funeral director, who I have known since the second grade, gave me an urn that supposedly contained her ashes. I have a death certificate from the state of Kentucky.

Despite all of that, Lamb claims to have talked to her on June 21st.

Thanks to MBNA and their collector—the ironically named, True Logic Financial Corporation—mom is now in a category with Elvis Presley, Kurt Cobain, and Jim Morrison. She has been deemed alive despite tremendous evidence to the contrary.

Mom would love being associated with Elvis but would not have been wild about being categorized with Kurt and Jim.

It seems almost comical now, but I was really angry. My mother died without warning, and I miss her. If MBNA's collector is able to talk to her, I wish he would give me her number.

The story of my mom and MBNA is an example of why credit card companies need more regulation.

I was named administrator of mom's estate after she supposedly died. I then received a letter saying MBNA had obtained an arbitration award against mom.

No one in my family knew anything about a debt to MBNA. Mom was supposedly dead, so we could not ask her.

I hired a lawyer to contact MBNA and to give us some verification of the alleged debt and arbitration award. Two months went by with no response. The attorney followed up again, but MBNA never got back to us.

Instead of responding to my attorney, MBNA shifted the alleged debt to True Logic.

Taking MBNA and True Logic at their word, I'm curious as to what mom said to Mr. Lamb. I hope they have a tape recording. Mom was known to use salty language, and I'm sure Mr. Lamb would have heard some.

I'm not as prone to foul language, but if MBNA ever calls me, I am going to make an exception.

After True Logic sent the letter for MBNA, I once again hired an attorney, and once again he sent a letter denying the alleged debt.

If MBNA wants to sue, I am not sure if they will go after the estate or have mom declared "un-dead" since they are having conversations with her. I'm not sure how to proceed if mom orally agreed to a payment plan. A judge will have to figure all that out.

The whole incident has made me wonder how often MBNA ignores the legal right of creditors to verify a debt. They have one collector send a letter, ignore the response, and then have another collector try again.

I suspect that collectors can sometimes convince an unsuspecting family or estate to pay money.

The first letter from MBNA sounded serious. It was enough for me to hire a lawyer. The only follow up I received from MBNA was the letter from Mr. Lamb saying he spoke to a woman who is legally dead.

On the other hand, it could be that Lamb did talk to mom. One of her favorite movies was *Ghost*. Mom may not be able to communicate with me, but Lamb might be a real-life version of the psychic that Whoopi Goldberg portrayed in the movie. By talking to Lamb, Mom may be sending a signal that she wants MBNA to put up or shut up.

Mom is one you never wanted to mess with; allegedly dead or allegedly alive.

# Credit Card Czar

*"When all your promises are gone; I'm the only one."*

**—Melissa Etheridge**

An MBNA collector claimed to have talked to my mother on June 21, 2006, even though she had died on April 2nd.

I've found that MBNA is not the only credit card company communicating with the dead. I've heard several collection stories worse than mine.

If you want to get rich, handing out credit cards is a good business to be in. Randy Lerner, the former chairman of MBNA, is a billionaire who owns the Cleveland Browns football team. He sold MBNA to Bank of America for a pot load of money.

After he hit a billion, you'd think he would have left my dead mother alone.

I can understand trying to collect from people who owe you.

It's different when you try to collect from people who don't owe you. Forty-two percent of complaints made to the Federal Trade Commission claim that collectors have gone after the wrong person or demanded extra money.

That doesn't even count post-mortem collections from people like mom.

I filed a complaint against MBNA. The problem is there is not one place to complain. I sent letters to the Federal Trade Commission, the Comptroller of the Currency, various state Attorney Generals, and various state consumer protection agencies.

I've spent my life in the financial services industry. If I can't figure out where to complain, I can't imagine how a blue-collar worker could get to the right place.

We need a credit card czar.

Consumers need one agency, one address, and one phone number to call about abusive credit card companies and collectors.

That credit card czar should have some real authority. None of the above mentioned agencies have any power. The web site for the Federal Trade Commission basically tells you not to expect their help, and the Comptroller of the Currency is usually a banking industry lapdog. State agencies don't have the resources to go after billion-dollar credit card companies.

You can see why the former MBNA chair can afford to buy sports teams.

It is a wonderful time to be a collector. Laws are rarely enforced, and fines are low.

A credit card czar would keep the abuses in check. A czar could issue a license to be a collector. Anyone that goes over the line could be thrown out of the collection's business.

Even without a credit card czar, there are some ways to reign in abuses.

One place to look would be state bar associations.

A trend in law firms nowadays is to have few lawyers on staff but an army of collectors who operate under their umbrella.

To me, the solution is simple. If a "law firm" cannot manage or supervise their staff, the partners in the firm should be disbarred. If that happened a couple of times, collectors would not go over the line as often as they do now.

At the very least, they would stop claiming to talk to dead people.

# Sucker Money and Credit Score Insanity

*"I hope that it's only amnesia. Believe me; I'm sick, but not insane."*

**—Pousette-Dart Band**

People often ask me personal finance questions.

The most common is how to improve their credit history score.

If you need to improve your credit score, it means you have lousy credit. Before trying to fix the score, people need to ask themselves how their credit got so bad to begin with.

Some would be better off not having access to credit at all; they can't handle it.

I'm not talking about people who got behind because of medical bills, life emergencies, or unemployment. Those are people with a good credit history who have had something bad happen to them. They deserve a second chance.

I'm focused on the other category: people who spend beyond their means or spend money on stupid stuff.

I don't want those people to have access to credit; if they do, they will get in trouble again.

They need to figure out how they got into trouble the first time.

They need to look at themselves and understand some basic principles about finance.

I tell people to spend less, pay for things in cash, start budgeting, and write down all of their expenditures.

Many need to learn the difference between needs and wants. People need food, clothing, and shelter. They don't need the latest video game.

Yet oftentimes, when it comes to those extravagancies, they never really wanted the items that badly in the first place; they just wanted it to keep up appearances.

People often get into trouble trying to keep up with friends and neighbors who also make stupid spending decisions.

Once that spiral starts, it rarely stops. Those who are caught up in it spend their lives trying to keep ahead of creditors.

They think that getting more credit is their answer.

My advice rarely goes anywhere, particularly with those out to impress their buddies.

It reminds me of a scene in the movie *Saturday Night Fever* where Tony's boss tells him to think about the future. Tony says, "**** the future." The boss responds, "if you say **** the future, the future will **** you."

Few would draw philosophical insights from a film like *Saturday Night Fever*. Yet Tony's remark is a good example of the kind of attitude people have when they come to me for credit score help. They blow money every weekend and have no long-range plan.

Gamblers have a term for people with that type of financial outlook: suckers. They call the money that these people spend "sucker money."

There are a lot of suckers out there. Likewise, there are a lot of people who want to take advantage of them.

If you have a lousy credit rating, there are a host of sub-prime lenders, high-interest credit card issuers, check cashing companies, and payday lenders dying to get their hands on you. They will give you more debt and more bills to pay.

A cottage industry has developed among companies claiming they can improve people's credit scores.

I've never seen these companies achieve any real success. They prey on suckers looking for quick and easy solutions. Since the companies charge a hefty fee for their services, they get debtors even further into debt.

There are two simple ways to improve your credit score: one is to pay your bills on time and the other is to not have as many debts. If you don't have many creditors, it is easy to handle what debt you have.

I give that advice often and then watch people's eyes glaze over.

If I were to turn evil and offer them an easy credit fix or a payday loan, I'd become a billionaire.

It is not easy to get people to take a hard look at themselves. Addiction to credit is like any addiction. People usually won't get help until they bottom out.

When people with poor credit get themselves together, they often get amnesia about what got them in trouble. They make the same mistakes over and over.

That is not amnesia; that is insanity.

# Credit Card Overlords

*"We come from the land of the ice and snow; from the midnight sun where the hot springs blow...of how we calmed the tides of war; we are your overlords."*

**—Led Zeppelin**

The Capital One credit card company uses actors portraying Vikings in its commercials. The Vikings bemoan the evils of high interest credit cards.

The Capital One commercials downplay the fact that Capital One makes money by getting people hooked on high-interest debt.

It is like an OxyContin dealer criticizing people who sell heroin.

January is the toughest time of year for people with credit cards. People go crazy during the holidays and come into a new year with heavy debt.

The credit card companies become their overlords.

The credit card companies are out to make a profit. They found millions of weak and gullible people who use credit cards instead of paying in cash.

It is hard to get mad at the companies. They target a segment of America who is convinced they can't live without the latest gadget. The credit card companies loan them money at a high price.

In the old days, people called high-interest lenders "loan sharks." Now, the business has gotten more respectable. The terms of the loans have not changed, but the lenders are billion-dollar institutions instead of guys on street corners.

Credit card companies don't hire leg breakers; although some credit card phone collectors would be good in that profession.

Like the loan sharks of old, credit card companies target people who want instant gratification.

Several years ago, I read a book called *Christians in the Marketplace* by Bill Hybels, the founder of the Willow Street Church in Chicago.

Hybels said that if your work is focused on paying for a car or material possession, the car or possession takes the place of God in your life.

In attracting the masses, Hybels would have more parishioners if he co-marketed with the credit card people.

Credit card companies have more converts than any other faith. Billy Graham and his crusades did not attract the crowds that Capital One does.

I understand people with poor cash flow getting hooked on credit cards. Some people use them to buy groceries. When I started my business, I used credit cards to make the payroll and keep the utilities from being shut off. When you are in survival mode, you do what you have to do.

Many people who get sucked into the credit card trap are not poor. They are hard working people who can't handle money.

I have a friend who works at a high-paying factory job. His wife works in the same factory and their family income is over $100,000.

They had to file bankruptcy. They made big money, but they were suckers for new vehicles and for all kinds of electronic equipment.

Their Gods became Toyota and Best Buy.

I know lots of people like my friends. They have a tremendous work ethic, but can't stay ahead of their bills.

I'm not sure how to break the cycle. Some people break it when their credit gets cut off, but my friends always get credit. After they filed bankruptcy, they got more offers than ever.

I don't like the credit card companies targeting weak-willed people, but those people need to take responsibility for bad behaviors.

The idea of buying a slightly used car, or waiting a couple of years for a 60-inch plasma television set, is foreign to them. They want the newest and the best and want it now.

The credit card companies allow them to do it at a heavy price.

If the people would save instead of paying credit card interest, they would soon have the money to buy what they want. They could then own it free and clear.

The Vikings came from the land of ice and snow and enslaved people with physical violence. Credit card companies enslave people with high interest and payment plans.

Vikings took people by force. People with credit cards do it voluntarily.

Millions of people surrender to the credit card overlords.

# Bankruptcy Court: Playground for the Rich

*"Cause if my eyes don't deceive me, there's something going wrong around here."*

**—Joe Jackson (Sugar Ray)**

In 2005, Congress made a move mislabeled as "bankruptcy reform." Credit card companies convinced Congress to pass laws that made it almost impossible for people to file chapter seven bankruptcies.

Instead of getting a fresh start, people are sent to a mini version of debtors' prison. They have to work out extended payment plans, go through mandatory "credit counseling," and are never really allowed a chance to get back on their feet.

While Congressmen and credit card lobbyists espouse the evils of debt, the credit card companies might as well hand out credit cards on street corners.

It blows my mind that college students and people with no income get credit cards. Almost every car dealer advertises how you can get a car with poor credit or bad credit. I keep waiting for Rolls Royce and Ferrari to have their "fresh restart" plans. There is a whole world of "sub-prime" lenders who will give money to just about anyone.

The fees and interests rates are scandalous, and banks are raking in billions. People who shouldn't get credit are in way over their heads.

After giving credit to people who should never get it, finance companies were horrified that people weren't paying it back.

My father was a bookmaker and professional gambler. Unlike the movie stereotype, bookmakers don't have many options if someone skips out on a bet. They cut the bettor off and write off the loss as bad experience.

Bookies figured that out. The bankers ran to Congress instead.

Bankruptcy reform had a place if it had been part of a bigger lending reform package. If Congress had reined in the abusive lending, fees, and collections practices of credit card companies, it would be fair to add tougher bankruptcy laws.

That did not happen. The debtors were punished, but the creditors are still collecting high interest rates and huge fees.

It is like passing a drug enforcement law that tortures users while giving economic incentives to pushers.

Bankruptcy court has never been a friendly place. Bankruptcy has a stigma and effect on a person's credit for years. My first office was in the same building as a bankruptcy court. The people always looked beaten down and overwhelmed by life.

There are some happy people coming to bankruptcy courts; the CEO's of big companies.

There is no stigma for a big company filing bankruptcy. It has become a smart business strategy. You look like a fool if you don't do it.

Big airlines like Delta, United, and US Air have made the rounds through Chapter Eleven bankruptcy. They used bankruptcy laws to dump union contracts and drop long term leases.

Most appalling are businesses using bankruptcy laws to dump their pensions and health insurance for retired workers.

The workers and businesses had an understanding. The businesses told the workers that if you devote your life to our company, we will make sure that you and your families are taken care of.

Now the companies are trying to wiggle out of the deal; Congress let them do it.

Those Members of Congress who talk tough about debtors are quieter when the deadbeat is a big coal company or airline.

Coal companies and airlines have better lobbyists than bankrupt, working people.

Bankruptcy courts have become a playground for big corporations and finance companies.

If my eyes don't deceive me, there is something going wrong around here.

# The Credit Counseling Crackdown

*"Lightning striking again, and again, and again, and again."*

—Lou Christie

It is rare for lightening to strike in the same place twice.

The same holds true for Internal Revenue Service (IRS) audits. Each time the IRS audits a different organization, using different auditors, in different parts of the country, it is going to come out with different results.

That is why I found a *Washington Post* article incredible.

The article in the *Post* reported that the IRS has audited forty-one alleged non-profit organizations that offer credit counseling services, and in ALL forty-one cases, the IRS recommended that the organizations' tax exempt status be revoked.

Think about it for a second. Forty-one times in forty-one different places, the IRS did an audit and all forty-one auditors concluded that the IRS needed to take severe action.

I do not think there is something wrong with the IRS. However, I think there is something wrong with the "non-profit" credit counseling industry.

Taking away the tax exempt status is the IRS' version of the death penalty. No tax exempt organization is going to operate as a tax paying company and survive.

Not one of the forty-one companies came away with a clean audit or a slap on the wrist. If the IRS cannot find one single organization that is doing it right, then we need to forget about the current system and start from scratch.

This is not an industry with a problem. This is an industry that needs to be shut down.

Although shutting down "non-profit" credit counseling sounds like a good idea, there is a small problem. Congress added a bonehead clause to the "bankruptcy reform" legislation. The clause REQUIRES anyone wanting to file bankruptcy to spend money on credit counseling.

Because of the new law, people are being forced into credit counseling and as a result, paying big money for it. Obviously, they are not getting what they paid for.

The same article said the IRS has begun criminal investigations. I hope every U.S. Attorney puts it on the top of his prosecution list.

Credit counseling companies were supposedly set up to help the poorest and the most desperate get out of debt. Instead, Congress has forced these debtors to become prey.

There is no reason for people near bankruptcy to seek credit counseling, even if the credit counselors are on the up and up. There have been some allegations that credit counselors receive fees from banks issuing credit cards, and that going to a credit counselor counts against a person's credit score.

A person thinking about bankruptcy needs to talk to lawyer who works for them and them alone.

It is obvious that the credit counseling people must have had great lobbyists working for them. My company would make more money if Congress forced people to come to me, but few industries get the sweet deal that the credit counseling people got.

The whole "bankruptcy reform" bill is an example of Congress at its worst. The bill was not designed to help working class people or small businesses; it was a bill designed to let the richest credit card issuers get richer.

It was welfare for billion-dollar companies. It was also welfare for the Congressmen who received big campaign contributions from the credit card issuers.

Poor people do not attend $1000-a-person political fundraisers unless they are there to wash the dishes afterwards.

Since the "bankruptcy reform" was one of the few triumphs in the second term for the Bush administration, the credit counseling companies cannot claim the IRS audits are political persecution.

What happens to the people who are laid off or ill and need to file bankruptcy? The law says they need to go back to the same clowns that the IRS is shutting down.

Now that the IRS' record is forty-one for forty-one in audits, I wonder what will happen if they audit every single company that is in the credit counseling business.

If they do, I suspect that lightening will keep striking again, and again, and again.

# Section Eleven

# Winners and Losers in the Worlds of Addiction

# Al Smith: Winning the Battle against Alcohol

# Al Smith, Steven Tyler, and Amazing

*"It's amazing; with the blink of an eye you finally see the light. It's amazing; when the moment arrives that you know you'll be alright."*

**—Steven Tyler & Aerosmith**

The lyrics of "Amazing" are touching; especially if you know the story of Tyler's battle with heroin addiction.

He fought his demons and he beat them.

Kentucky television commentator and publisher, Al Smith, fought a battle with alcohol. Forty years ago, he beat it.

SON OF A SON OF A GAMBLER

People like Al and Steven Tyler see the light and recognize the greatness within them.

A lot of people battle different demons. I've never been big on drinking or drugs, but I fight compulsive eating. I started a Fat Guys group (now Get-Fit group) in Richmond, Kentucky, and we have lost weight together.

Sometimes it takes a group to help someone see the light.

Other people can help those in the dumps to recognize their self-worth.

The movie *It's a Wonderful Life* hammers home the idea that one person can have an impact on those around them.

People need positive affirmation; especially those who are battling addictions, life changes, or depression.

They need to know that they add value to the world.

Tyler wrote "Amazing" after he got his life together, and the band made a huge comeback. They are now icons of the music world.

There is nothing worse than seeing a friend or loved one in the grips of a demon like drugs, alcohol, or depression. They feel helpless, and you feel helpless wanting them to "snap out of it."

It's something that people have to do for themselves. There has to be something that shakes their life so that they see the light. It has to come from within.

It does help when someone has empathy for your problem. I've never been around Steven Tyler, but Al Smith is a father figure to me. I turn to him when I need sage advice, and I know he truly cares about me.

One of the reasons we connected is that we have both battled addiction, and as a recovering alcoholic, he has a perspective that commands my respect. I am not a particularly good listener, but I listen when he talks.

He has not walked my exact walk, but he certainly knows the neighborhood.

In one of my first conversations with Al, I immediately asked him how he stopped drinking. It was an extremely personal question to ask someone I just met, but I suspected Al would want to talk about it; he did. Being open is part of how he keeps the demons away.

Al devotes his life to helping people. He has had tremendous success as a journalist and businessman, but what really makes him happy is pushing other people along.

Al is constantly sending my stuff to every person who might read it. He also sends me articles from every other journalist he is helping.

We are all part of the big Al Smith journalistic family. I have more brothers and sisters than John-Boy Walton.

Al is like a real-life version of the *It's a Wonderful Life* movie. He plays the role of Clarence the Angel who got his wings by helping George Bailey (Jimmy Stewart's character) recognize his worth.

In the story, Bailey had done so much for his community, but he needed Clarence to point it out for him.

People battling demons need a Clarence in their lives. It also helped that Clarence had some flaws himself and experience with what Bailey was going through.

It can't be easy for someone like Steven Tyler or Al Smith to talk about their problems, but they know they will spark other people to see the light.

Desperate hearts can then see that someone else has fought the same demons and won.

It's Amazing.

# Al Smith and Drunken Angels

*"Drunken Angel; you're on the other side."*

**—Lucinda Williams**

I understand what it is like to be addicted, but I don't understand what causes addiction. My best guess is that obesity, alcoholism, and drug addiction are part of your genetic makeup.

My family hit the obesity gene 100%. Everyone battled their weight.

I understand being compulsive and addicted. Because life seems out of control, probably every addicted person wants to give up the struggle. I've watched addicts fall off the wagon over and over again. I sometimes think attempts at rehabilitation are futile.

Then I see my friend Al Smith.

Al is one of Kentucky's most famous and celebrated journalists. After over thirty years of hosting *Comment on Kentucky,* on Kentucky Educational Television, he has become a universally known and beloved figure.

He is certainly my role model. We have a deep bond, yet what I really admire about him is that somehow, forty years ago, the drunken Al Smith stumbled into an Alcoholics Anonymous meeting in Russellville, Kentucky and turned his life around.

He's never been able to explain how he chose that time and that moment to break the hold of alcohol. All I know is that he did it.

Like me, Al is not reserved when it comes to sharing information from his life. I was watching the close-out for a Thanksgiving show when he briefly stated that he had been an alcoholic. He went on to speak about The Healing Place, a recovery center in Louisville.

I checked out The Healing Place's web site, http://www.thehealingplace.org, and it is impressive. They have a recovery rate of 65%, which is five times the national average.

Someone close to me battled alcohol addiction for most of her short life. She was never able to walk through the door of a recovery center like The Healing Place.

That is what impresses me about Al Smith: not that he remained sober for 40 years, but rather that he made the initial decision to walk through the door of that Russellville church and get help.

I think his success was partly due to the fact that he lived in a small town. Almost all United States Presidents, with Teddy Roosevelt a notable exception, grew up in small towns. They developed a sense of community and hard work.

I understand the rooted feeling that a small town gives. I grew up five miles from downtown Cincinnati but still within the limits of a small city called Edgewood, Kentucky. When I went away to college, I knew almost all of Edgewood's 5,000 residents.

When my mother and my sister died, people came to the funerals that I had not seen in thirty years. We had that small-town sense of connection that is impossible to lose.

I don't know if researchers tie addiction to being socially disconnected, but there has to be a correlation. Addiction comes from genetics and possibly environmental factors, but groups like Alcoholics Anonymous are fueled by love. What works is the connection and support of the group.

I started a group for overweight men. Even better than The Healing Place, we have a 100% record of people losing weight. We don't do anything special or fancy. We just show up each week and support each other.

My drunken angel is on the other side. I want to stop others from taking that same journey.

# Fat Guys and Fit Guys

# Sunday Morning Coming Down

*"Well I woke up Sunday morning, with no way to hold my head that didn't hurt; and the beer I had for breakfast wasn't bad, so I had one more for desert."*

**—Kris Kristofferson (Johnny Cash)**

On New Year's Day there were many people with Sunday morning hangovers. For some people, it happens once a year. For others, it is an every day experience.

Many people use booze or drugs when life is out of control. It is easier to pop a pill or have a beer, than to tackle one's underlying problems.

New Year's is a time when people make life changes. Diet classes and workout centers fill up every January, and people make resolutions to improve themselves.

My demon is my weight.

A few years ago, I started a group called Don's Get Fit Club. I wrote a column inviting overweight men in the community to come meet me and share ideas about losing weight. Four men showed up, and the group was started.

The group is still going strong. We've added a few members (and are looking for more), but every person in the group has lost weight.

The Get Fit Guys have been an amazing success story.

Like most successful self-help groups, we do not charge a fee; we simply give each other support.

We are different from 12-step groups in that we are competitive. Every week, we each put a dollar in a pot, and the person who reports the most weight loss gets the cash. It is a motivator. I won three weeks in a row, and everyone was gunning for me on the fourth.

Motivation is the key to battling demons. I don't know what makes a person decide to get help, but it has to come from within. Once they decide, they need the support of others and from a higher power.

People who turn to booze, drugs, and other poisons use them as a substitute for something missing in their lives.

Employees with substance abuse problems create a real dilemma. In the past, I've had good employees suddenly become bad employees when faced with a trauma in their personal lives. They started drinking or taking medications.

It was not just Sunday morning coming down, it was Monday, Tuesday, and every other day as well. They were constantly hung over.

They did not come to work drunk or stoned, but they were clearly not at the top of their game either. Although we cared for them as people, the organization couldn't carry someone who was not pulling their weight.

It is not easy to suggest that someone should start dealing with their problems. Most people with problems know they have problems. They don't appreciate you pointing it out to them.

You don't need to tell me I'm fat. My scale, clothes, and broken chair will do that for me.

On the other hand, if you are a true friend, you want to get the person to confront their issues. Concern needs to be communicated in an effective manner.

I once suggested to a friend via email that she needed to find a therapist. I had good intentions with bad implementation.

If I had received the e-mail instead of sending it, I would have responded by sending the lyrics to the Aaron Tippin song "Kiss This."

My friend had a milder temperament.

A struggling person needs support from other people. That is one of the reasons that groups like Alcoholics Anonymous have had tremendous success. They give members love and understanding.

The Get Fit Guys works because we root for each other and yet maintain a competitive nature.

I hope people fighting drug and alcohol problems will use the next New Year as an opportunity to examine their lives and battle their demons.

It could be the last year that they face another Sunday morning coming down.

# The $40 Billion Search for Weight Loss Bliss

*"Oh Lord, won't you buy me a Mercedes Benz. My friends all drive Porsches; I must make amends."*

—Janis Joplin

I don't want the Lord to buy me a Mercedes Benz. I had one that always broke down.

I want a magic potion to make me thin.

According to Somerset, Kentucky psychologist Dr. Tammy Hatfield, I am not alone. Americans spend over $40 billion per year on diets and diet products.

Where I come from, $40 BILLION is a lot of money. Most of it is wasted. Ninety-five percent of dieters gain the weight back.

I've done every crash diet there is—liquid diets, Atkins diets, and diets that I made up as I went along. Like the other 95% of Americans, I put it back on and then some.

The crash system has not worked.

I've lost significant weight since I started Don's Get Fit Club (formally Don's Fat Guy Club) as a support group in Richmond, Kentucky. We focus on better eating habits and exercise.

It's slow and painful, but it works. Nothing else does. I intellectually know that fads are a waste of money. Even after having watched friends die from taking prescription weight-loss medicines, I am still a sucker for a quick fix.

I want something that will take my weight off quickly. I've never really focused on why.

Dr. Hatfield, who has lectured extensively and written about eating disorders, said that Americans waste money in an effort to realize a difficult and often unattainable goal.

They want to look like George Clooney or Angelina Jolie.

I know George Clooney's parents. They are great-looking and gave him their genetic code. My parents gave me mine. It is not the same code.

No one has ever mistaken me for George. They may mistake George for me, but I don't hear about it.

There are health-related reasons to lose weight, and it is therefore not surprising that the real solutions point back to a healthier lifestyle. Eating less and exercising more will create both a healthy and attractive body, and it will provide lifelong benefits.

Think about it. Doing a crash diet to become healthy is insane. The short-term weight loss can cause long-term problems.

I'd feel better if dieters were truly motivated by health. I don't think they are. Many are motivated by media images and the corporations making $40 billion a year off our failed efforts.

Wait until January. Weight-loss commercials will run nonstop, and millions will rush to try the newest fad. By February, the diets will be over, the money wasted, and the weight loss turned into a gain.

There is a point at which some people get off the cycle—when the attempt to lose weight kills them.

Some of my friends have died after taking "miracle" diet medicines like Redux or Fen-Phen. They were not obese; they were trying to lose a few extra pounds.

The "miracle" diet drugs that The Food and Drug Administration approved caused people to die a horrible death. After many fatalities, the FDA banned the medications that they never should have approved.

Now, there is a new "miracle" diet drug being used in other countries. Despite the previous diet-drug deaths, it will be in America soon. The drug companies can make billions, and the FDA is a toothless lapdog. No one is going to stop it.

I hope fewer people die this time.

I was a big fan of Karen Carpenter. I never dreamed that she had any kind of problems, especially involving her weight; She did.

She became the most famous victim of anorexia. The pressures to stay thin killed her.

Weight loss was not about her health, it was about personal and public perception; as it is for many people.

I really don't want the Lord to send me a Mercedes Benz. A Mercedes seems wonderful, but owning one never worked for me.

A magic weight-loss potion also seems wonderful, but I suspect it won't work for me either.

# Mike Huckabee: Former Fat Guy for President

*"Don't stop thinking about tomorrow."*

**—Fleetwood Mac**

"Don't Stop" was the theme song of Arkansas Governor Bill Clinton's presidential campaign. Another Arkansas Governor is running for president, Republican Mike Huckabee.

Huckabee and Clinton have different ideologies, but thinking about tomorrow is their common message.

President Clinton, Governor Huckabee, and I have all fought obesity. Clinton solved his weight problem after emergency bypass heart surgery.

Not a great strategy.

Huckabee did it by losing 100 pounds in a medically-supervised weight loss program. He kept it off and has since become a national model for how to battle obesity.

I need to lose as much as Governor Huckabee did.

I lost 90 pounds in 1989 but did not keep it off. After recently reading Huckabee's book, *Quit Digging Your Grave with a Knife and Fork,* I saw where I screwed up.

When I lost the weight, I thought I was cured. I thought I would never be fat again.

I was wrong.

I fell back into old eating patterns. I gained about a pound a week.

If you gain a pound a week for two years, you gain 104 pounds, and that's exactly what happened to me.

Huckabee made a subtle but important point: obesity is treatable, not curable. Like people addicted to alcohol or drugs, food addicts need to always be in a stage of recovery.

I don't think everyone gets that. Unlike alcohol or drugs, food is not something you swear off completely.

The key is to replace bad habits with good habits. Fast food restaurants have to be replaced with healthy eating and exercise.

Huckabee's personal wake-up call was a diagnosis of diabetes. He did not set out to lose a specific number of

pounds. He wanted to get his blood pressure, choles-
terol, and blood sugar back to normal levels.

His motivation was to add years to his life.

Huckabee made me realize that battling obesity is a
journey that has no end.

The alternative is an early grave.

Insurance companies offer something called "rated-age"
annuities.

To get people to understand them, I explain that these
annuities ratings are the mirror opposite of life insurance. People have to pay more for their life insurance if
they smoke, skydive, or do things that reduce how long
they might live.

Rated-age annuities work the other way. Insurance
companies invest a lump sum and send person money
for the rest of their lives. They will give an unhealthy
person more each month than a healthy one. They don't
plan on the unhealthy person being around as long.

I recently gathered my medical records and applied to
several companies for a rated-age annuity.

The consensus was that I would die at age 68. Unless I
end my obesity, I will die about nine years sooner than
other men my age.

That was a serious wake-up call. The insurance company actuaries and medical underwriters have billions
of dollars riding on their research, and they are usually
accurate.

The only way to prove them wrong is to lose weight and change my lifestyle.

I went back to the medically-supervised program and got a personal trainer.

My politics are probably closer to Clinton, but Huckabee seems like my kind of guy. He is a recovering fat guy and likes rock and roll. He can't be all bad. Having battled and treated obesity, he will not stop thinking about tomorrow.

# Fat, Drunk, and Stupid is No Way to Go through Life

*"Fat, drunk, and stupid is no way to go through life, son."*

**—Dean Wormer in the movie *Animal House***

I've been fat most of my life but not recently drunk.

Stupid is in the eye of the beholder.

It is obvious that some people who run fast food restaurants think that fat people are stupid. More and more people are trying low-carbohydrate diets, and fast food restaurants are trying to cash in the craze.

Some restaurants make a real effort. They create or modify menu items that fit into low-carbohydrate diets and try to develop choices for people following those programs.

Others are a little more annoying. Rather than develop some new menu items, they proudly advertise that they will serve their sandwiches without the bread to accommodate their dieting customers.

They assume that fat people are either too stupid to take the meat off the bread themselves or so weak-willed that they will immediately gobble up any bread they can get their hands on. They don't charge less for "sandwiches" without the bread, even though the restaurant is making more money off the dieter. Also, it takes away the opportunity for the dieter to give the bread to a hungry person or starving bird who might appreciate the gesture.

Since I know what is healthy and what is not, I get irritated when restaurant chains present high-calorie, high-carbohydrate, and high-fat foods as being good for you. My favorite example was when KFC started advertising that their chicken is better for you than a Burger King Whopper.

I suspect that there is nothing worse for you than eating a Whopper. It is high-fat, high-carbohydrate, and high calorie but tastes extremely good. Eating pure lard or a pound of sugar might be healthier than downing a Whopper.

It was very annoying for KFC to advertise that their stuff has some kind of health value. They didn't compare their menu to a vegetarian co-op. Putting KFC up against the Whopper was probably the only way they could possibly market themselves as a healthy alternative to other fast-food joints.

It is like telling someone who is an alcoholic that switching from pure-grain alcohol to just drinking vodka would be a good move. The effect will still be the same: drunkenness.

Speaking of being drunk, several beer companies have starting pushing the low-carbohydrate qualities of their products too. They make it seem like knocking back a 12-pack is downright healthy.

When I was a child, there were a number of hard-drinking men in my neighborhood who developed what were called beer bellies. I have one myself, except mine came from fast food and soft drinks.

In the world of beer commercials, beer seems to turn men into slim, muscle-bound guys. Supermodels rip off their clothes whenever they see me.

The men in my neighborhood drank a lot of beer but looked lousy. No one took their clothes off around them—not even their wives.

I guess they were drinking the wrong brand.

My neighbors might have been considered fat, drunk, and stupid, but there's one thing I am sure of: they didn't think of fried chicken or Whoppers as health foods.

# The FDA: Not Good Enough for Government Work

*"Everything you think, do, and say is in the pill you took today."*

**—Zager and Evans ("In the Year 2525")**

*The New England Journal of Medicine* showcased an article entitled, "Good Enough for Government Work," by Harvard Medical School Professor Jerry Avorn M.D.

It is critical of the Food and Drug Administration.

The phrase "good enough for government work" implies that the government has lower standards than private industry.

Government standards ought to be higher than private business. Government is funded by all Americans and was created to help people.

The FDA ought to have especially high standards: they deal in life and death.

The FDA is supposed to be our watchdog, but it maybe the pharmaceutical industry's lapdog.

You see many stories about the FDA getting cozy with the drug companies that they are supposed to be regulating.

People at the FDA need to remember that they are messing with people's lives.

Several of my friends died because the FDA allowed drugs like Redux onto the market.

They took drugs because the FDA said they were safe; they were not.

I don't know how bureaucrats who make decisions that killed people can sleep at night.

I guess they load up on the new insomnia pills.

Avorn discussed how the FDA needs to distinguish between "lifestyle" and "live-saving" drugs.

The big money for the drug companies is in "lifestyle" drugs.

Since there are men who'll pay big money for Viagra, and a demand for weight-loss pills, there is a big incentive for drug companies to give people what they want.

Just look at their television advertising. You don't see ads for pills that save lives.

The companies spend their advertising dollars on pills to help your sex life.

There are millions who want to romp around like people in the Levitra and Cialis ads. There are only a limited number of people who need to buy cancer drugs.

The FDA ought to focus their attention on approving lifesaving drugs. You hear stories of people going to foreign countries for medicine because the FDA is too slow to approve drugs that could be vital to their health.

That should never happen.

If a drug allows a person to live longer, the FDA ought to act quickly to make sure it gets to the people who need it.

Conversely, lifestyle drugs should not come on the market until the FDA is sure that they WON'T kill somebody.

The promise of billions of dollars in profits led the pharmaceutical companies to push diet drugs onto the market before they were proven safe. Their friends in the FDA let it happen.

Ed Norton's character in the movie *Fight Club* was a guy who worked for an automobile manufacturer. His job was to try and figure out if it was cheaper to recall a defective product or to stay quiet and try to settle any injury claims that come up.

I suspect that a similar decision-making process goes on at drug companies. They walk a line between ensuring big profits and doing things carefully in a manner that saves lives.

Without proper regulation and oversight, the companies are going to fall to the temptation of quick money. There is too much pressure from stockholders and competitors.

It is the FDA's job to keep the drug companies in line.

We also need to focus on avoiding the use of lifestyle drugs.

I have a terrible time controlling my weight, and I am always looking for a quick answer. I took Redux and would be tempted by another diet pill like it.

It would be simpler than switching to proper diet and exercise.

A doctor told me that people are falling into the trap that Elvis Presley did, where he needed pills to wake up, sleep, and get through the day.

Drug companies are pushing pills that can control everything we think, do, and say. We need the FDA to watch them.

We also need to think before we pop that next "lifestyle" drug.

# Knocking on Heaven's Door

*"Its getting dark, too dark too see; I feel like I'm knocking on heaven's door."*

—**Bob Dylan (Warren Zevon)**

Although "Knocking on Heaven's Door" is a Bob Dylan song, I associate it more with Warren Zevon.

When Zevon found out that he had inoperable lung cancer, he gathered his friends and his strength to put out a last album entitled *The Wind*. "Knocking on Heaven's Door" was Zevon's goodbye note to the world.

When one of my middle-aged clients died, I was stunned because she seemed healthy just a few days before.

It was not a complete shock as she had Primary Pulmonary Hypertension (PPH). The life expectancy for someone with PPH is around four years.

We were very different people. I am an upper-income, white guy in central Kentucky. She was a poor, African-American woman in a large urban city.

We had a common bond: we had both taken the same prescription diet drug. It killed her; I am still here.

Every time I meet someone with PPH, I know that I could be in their shoes.

The book, *Dispensing with the Truth*, by Alicia Mundy gives the history of diet drugs like Phen-Fen and Redux. Mundy explained how greed and government incompetence allowed drug companies to market products that kill people.

Few people knew that diet drugs could cause PPH; I did. My doctor and I carefully studied the drug company's and the FDA's research. From the available literature, we read that one in a million people would get PPH.

With the odds at a million to one, I took the drug. In realty, the odds of death were much higher.

It is hard to know the true number of people who die from PPH. It is rare and difficult to diagnose, so many die without knowing the cause. Most doctors just don't know what to look for. Many people who die from PPH are written off as fat people who had heart attacks.

The drugs have been off the market for years, but new cases of PPH show up. I live in fear that the medicine will someday kill me.

I bond with PPH victims since I could have been in their shoes—I may still be.

Unless a cure is found, there is very little chance that people with PPH will live to an old age.

Since PPH is not a well-known disease, it does not receive the research dollars that other diseases get.

Pharmaceutical companies should be forced to spend as much money curing the disease as they did marketing the diet pills. If they sold $50 billion worth of diet drugs, they need to put $50 billion into PPH research.

If a pill can cause the disease, maybe another pill can cure it.

The federal government told us that the drugs were safe when they were not—perhaps the government should foot the bill to repair the damage.

People are dying because of their mistake.

I'm tired of watching my friends die. I don't want to die myself.

I show no symptoms of PPH, but I never know when they could pop up.

Good people are dying a painful death because of greed and a government screw-up. It has to stop.

Unless a cure is found, the knock on heaven's door could be mine.

# *Ashley Judd and Other Kinds of Addicts*

# Ashley Judd: Addicted to Being Perfect

*"Everybody just wants to get high; sit and watch a perfect world go by. There's not much space between us; drugs or Jesus."*

**—Tim McGraw**

Ashley Judd appears to have a perfect life. She is a rich and famous actress who seems to do the right thing. You can find copies of her sister Wynonna's mug shot, but you won't find Ashley's.

When given the choice between drugs or Jesus, it seemed obvious which Judd sister would go which way, or so we thought.

Ashley revealed that the emotional distance between the two sisters was not far apart. What differed was how they presented themselves.

Wynonna's problems are public. She has battled addictions and has been honest about her fight. Ashley seems perfect. No one would dream that she had her own demons.

Both sisters were cut from the same cloth. They had a rough childhood and came from the same troubled family. Both sisters dealt with their unhappiness differently.

Everything about Wynonna cries out for help, whereas nothing about Ashley does.

Many families have a perfect child and a difficult one. It is hard to realize that both children have their own unique set of issues.

Being the sibling of a perfect child can be tough.

There is a scene in *Saturday Night Fever* where the parents of Tony Monaro (John Travolta's character) are ashamed when his older brother left the priesthood. Monaro tells his brother, "If you're not so good, then I'm not so bad."

The road to perfection has victims and collateral damage.

I have always connected to screwed-up people. Just like Wynonna, you can see that I have a problem with food. I understand people who have problems. I could not always relate to someone like Ashley.

I can now. She has problems. I have problems. Her sister has problems. We are all trying to solve them.

A recent issue of the *New York Times* had a great article about the search for an anti-addiction pill.

The author frames a "drugs or Jesus argument" but in a different manner than Tim McGraw.

There is a debate as to whether addiction is a biological or a psychological problem. If the problem is biological, pharmaceutical drugs might cure it. If the problem is psychological, counseling and support would be the best treatment.

After 100 years of effort, no miracle drug has come along.

Jesus has had better success in curing addictions. Alcoholics Anonymous, Overeaters Anonymous, and all 12-step groups have a faith-based component, and all ask people to gain strength from a higher power.

Naomi Judd had it right when she said, "Love Can Build a Bridge."

Addictions are a tough bridge to cross. Someone who gave up smoking 10 years ago told me that she is fighting an urge to start again. I don't smoke, so I don't understand. She doesn't understand why I can't quit going to McDonald's. I don't understand drinking to excess, and I don't understand a quest to be perfect.

Actually, I can understand the perfection thing. I am a situational perfectionist, as anyone who works with me can attest. Even though it puts tremendous stress on people, I've considered my perfection to be a positive trait. I'm sure Ashley felt the same way. Unlike with booze or drugs, there are societal rewards for remaining perfect, even if there are severe costs.

I have a friend who reminds me of Ashley. She seems perfect, but her greatest fear is public embarrassment. I'll bet Ashley had the same problem. Wynonna is probably like me. Public failure doesn't bother us because we have experienced it.

I've never had a mug shot, but if I ever get one, I will smile into the camera like Wynonna did.

I admire Ashley for telling the world about her struggles. For someone who has always striven to appear perfect, going public had to be difficult.

It will inspire others to look at their own problems.

Thus, it was the perfect thing to do.

# Rudolph Giuliani and the OxyContin People

*"Well, now if I were the President of this land; you know, I'd declare total war on the pusher man. God damn the pusher."*

**—Steppenwolf**

Rudolph Giuliani started his political career claiming to be tough on criminals.

In some cases he is—unless the criminals hire him to be their lawyer.

The people who make OxyContin did something horrible: they sold a drug they knew was addictive and acted like it wasn't.

The makers of OxyContin got off easy when they agreed to a $634.5 million fine. Three of their top executives have to do some community service. None have to do jail time.

It was a wimpy settlement by the federal government. People with one OxyContin pill in their pocket often serve jail time. The people making millions of those pills did not.

I wondered why the OxyContin makers got such a sweetheart deal. Then I saw that Rudolph Giuliani was their lawyer.

*The Washington Post* said that Giuliani met with government lawyers more than half a dozen times.

Giuliani personally met with the head of the federal Drug Enforcement Administration (DEA) when the DEA's Drug Diversion Office began a criminal investigation into the makers of OxyContin.

No wonder the OxyContin people got a sweetheart deal; Giuliani is not a guy government bureaucrats want to mess with.

Imagine yourself as a government official and Rudolph Giuliani walks in to negotiate with you. At the time, Giuliani was the frontrunner to be the Republican nominee for President of the United States.

As a bureaucrat, you are negotiating with a guy who might be your boss.

If a frontrunner for president of the United States wants a good deal for his clients, you are going to think hard before you say no.

The OxyContin makers may not have strong morals, but they do have brains. They hired one of the best lawyers money could buy.

The old Rudolph Giuliani would have loved to have gone after the OxyContin makers. Rudy got his start as a federal prosecutor and liked to go after white-collar types.

Here was the perfect situation for the old Rudy. You had a company that knew their drug would make people addicts. The company officers devised a plan to market OxyContin to as many people as possible.

The old Rudy would have shut down the company and thrown all the officers in jail.

The new Rudy cut his clients a sweet deal: no one spends a day in jail. The federal government considered the crime to be a misdemeanor like noodling.

The $634.5 million is a cost of doing business. It didn't hurt the company's stock price.

There are thousands of people addicted to OxyContin, and hundreds died.

When you see round ups of street dealers, many are addicts trying to feed their addiction. Many of those addictions wouldn't have happened if Giuliani's clients had not been greedy, reckless, and stupid.

A better punishment would be to make the company execs take their own product for a couple months and then kick the habit in a county jail cell.

It would give them an idea of what really happens.

The Steppenwolf song "The Pusher" is a graphic depiction of someone addicted. The character wants the President of the United States to declare war on pushers. That doesn't just mean rounding up junkies and street dealers; it means doing something about big pharmaceutical companies too.

When the OxyContin people go to meet their maker, I hope that the response they get is, "God damn the pusher." Eternal damnation is the only thing that would balance the scales of justice.

# The OxyContin Letters

*"When things go wrong, don't walk away; that will only make it harder."*

**—Robin Lane and the Chartbusters**

I wrote about how the makers of OxyContin agreed to a wimpy $634.5 million settlement with federal prosecutors.

Purdue Pharma, the makers of OxyContin, were selling an addictive drug. The top executives knew it was addictive, and the company sold almost $10 billion of the stuff.

Their lawyer, former New York Mayor Rudolph Giuliani, negotiated a plea that kept the people at Purdue from going to jail.

Giuliani cut a deal that street pushers would drool over. The fine is a small percentage of their sales, and the drug is still on the market.

In the language of the street pusher, the people at Purdue copped a plea, paid a fine, and went back on the street.

In the wake of the OxyContin executives' admission to committing a crime, Congressmen Hal Rogers of Kentucky and Frank Wolff of Virginia, made a reasonable request.

They want OxyContin to be prescribed only for severe pain, not moderate pain.

Amazingly, Purdue Pharma, the makers of OxyContin, fought Rogers and Wolff.

Instead of thanking God for Rudy's great connections, the people at Purdue want the FDA to keep ignoring the problem.

Here is something I can't ignore. After I wrote my columns, I started hearing from people all over the world.

A reader in Texas wrote the following:

> "My sister was very much addicted to Oxycontin that she was obtaining legally from her doctor. She was living with my 72-year-old mother as she was unable to hold a job. Her boyfriend was also addicted to various drugs. One night she refused to give him more of her Oxycontin, and he left to

later return and cut the throats of my mother and sister."

The OxyContin problem is not confined to the United States. A reader in Canada wrote:

> "My son was addicted to Oxycontin for about 3 years. He is 22 months clean now but only because he is on the methadone maintenance program. We live in a small town and have to travel 2 hours each way weekly for him to be urine tested and to see the doctor. He was hooked so hard core, it is amazing he is still alive. He is clean right now, but he is a totally different person, often filled with anger. In our town of 6,500 people the drug of choice among our kids is Oxycontin!"

Not everyone liked my column. A financial consultant in New York City called me a jerk but didn't specify why. Either he likes OxyContin or likes Giuliani; maybe both.

An Arizona reader told me his doctor had prescribed OxyContin for his back pain, but that the doctor was careful to explain that the drug could be addictive. Thus, the man used OxyContin without incident.

After reading horror story after horror story, I can't imagine a scenario where I would willingly take OxyContin. I can understand doing so only if you and your doctor weigh the risks and benefits.

For moderate pain there has to be a better solution than OxyContin. Even if the government just limited supply, it would be a big step forward.

It takes a lot of gall to keep fighting after your company and its top executives have agreed to a $634.5 million fine—not to mention the fact that everyone was well-connected enough to avoid jail time.

Purdue apparently has that kind of gall.

The people at Purdue admitted to willfully doing something that harmed people. They ought to do more than pay a fine; they ought to show leadership and clean up some of the mess they started.

Instead, they want the FDA's blessing to keep on selling OxyContin to people with moderate pain.

The people at Purdue need to realize that when things go wrong, you don't walk away.

That will only make it harder.

# Acknowledgments

*"You didn't have to make it like you did;*
*But you did, but you did;*
*And I thank you."*

—ZZ Top

Stu Bykofsky, the celebrated columnist for the *Philadelphia Daily News*, noted about my previous book, *The Unbridled World of Ernie Fletcher*, that, "If everyone who you mentioned in your acknowledgements buys a book, you will have a bestseller."

Stu, you are in this one. I will be waiting for your check.

Stu served with me on the Board of Directors on the National Society of Newspaper Columnists. I enjoyed the gig and loved the people. Several were important in making this book happen.

Dave Lieber, the "Yankee Cowboy" columnist for the *Fort Worth Star-Telegram* was a primary catalyst for this book. He provided me with a ton of information on how he published his outstanding book, *The Dog of My Nightmares*. I followed his advice verbatim, which included using Janet Long to design my book cover.

Dave, thank you. Unlike Stu, you'll get a free copy of the book; autographed too.

Bob Haught is a legend of Oklahoma journalism and my mentor on the NSNC board. Bob's book, *Now, I'm No Expert: On CATS and Other Mysteries of Life* was mentioned by Paul Harvey on his syndicated radio show.

Bob, if you can drop a word about me to Paul, there's an autographed book in it for you.

I'm going to take Stu's advice and not mention some of the people I acknowledged in the last book; however, I do need to again thank former NSNC President Suzette Martinez Standring. She is a dear friend and a great writer. I also want to mention NSNC Vice President Samantha Bennett, whose unique view of the world can make me roar with laughter.

Stu hosted an incredible 2007 NSNC convention in Philadelphia, but I had to miss it. My health turned bad so I stayed home, got in shape, and finished writing this book.

Now I have a finished book, excellent vital signs, and I am 55 pounds lighter. I did miss seeing Stu and the gang.

When I lose 100 pounds, I'm writing a book called Fat Guy to Fit Guy, and it will star Dr. Phil Hoffman, who is better known as "Babydaddy's" daddy. It will also star Dr. James Anderson at the University of Kentucky and his crack staff of nurses, physicians, and health educators. Special thanks go to Jennifer Alcala who has served as my personal health educator.

When it comes to fitness, the man to see is Steve Carroll, my personal trainer in Richmond, Ky. He is determined to make me into a picture of health and a middle-age sex symbol. We are doing better on the health part. I also want to thank the members of Don's Get Fit Club. If you are in Richmond on Tuesday nights, come and lose weight with us.

Although my dad and mother get plenty of ink in the book, I also want to mention my daughters, Gena and Angela; my son in law, Clay Bigler; and my grandson Abijah. I hit a jackpot larger than any Powerball when they came into my life. We all work together at McNay Settlement Group. Some people hire a great organization. I adopted one.

My nephew, Nick McNay, spent a lot of time with my dad for the first 9 years of his life. It made an impact and Nick has the courage and persistence of both his grandparents. My niece, Lyndsay Jo Francis, inherited her mother's genius-level intelligence and is on her way to greatness.

My stepmother, Lynn McNay, met dad as he was moving away from gambling and into the travel business. Lynn made dad a semi-model citizen. Dad completely adored her, and I couldn't have asked for a better stepmom. My step-sister, Dobie, was dad's loyal and loving daughter and visa versa.

This book would not have happened without Janice Clayton. She is a combination of intelligence and a great work ethic. She took over every facet of getting the book to publication. She coordinated, edited, re-edited, and made impossible deadlines look simple. I sincerely thank her.

I also need to thank Sara Zeigler, Chair of the Eastern Kentucky University Department of Government, for referring Janice to me. Sara has sent me several great students who became great employees.

Jonathan Moore edited a great deal of the book's copy and edited my previous book. Wendell Wilson, who I once called "The Bill Gates of Kentucky," continues to keep me on the cutting edge of technology.

I would like to say thank you to Janet Long for doing a tremendous job on the book's cover.

I reconnected with my childhood friend Connie (Taroski) Kreyling at my sister's funeral, and Connie has become a loyal friend and sounding board.

When we were in high school, Mike Behler and I ran into an employee of my father's named "Lucky". Mike asked if "Lucky" was named "Lucky" the way that fat people are sometimes named "Slim". Mike still has his astute powers of observation and remains one of my closest friends.

Many of my friends are mentioned throughout the chapters, but Pierce Hamblin, Judge Bill Clouse, Joni Jenkins, Harry Moberly, Mike Tucker, Whitney Greer, Lee Gentry, Larry Doker, Jeff Chasen, Donna Davis, Liz Kuniholm,  Ivan "Buzz" Beltz, David Grise, Tom Sweeney, Shelia Holdt, Jackie Collier, Peter Perlman, Chris Bogie, Joanne (Gadker) Terlau, Cindy Shrooni, Judge Joseph Lee and Carole Lee, Richard Hay, Phil Taliaferro, Dennis Pike,  Rhonda Hatfield-Jeffers, Jim Vanover, Wanda and Dr. Larry Dry, Keith Bartley, Rick Robinson, Bill Garmer, Tom Herren, Carroll Crouch, Yvonne Yelton, Chuck Adams, Ben and Jennifer Chandler, Jim Gray,  Joice Biazoto, Matt Harville, David and Connie Baird, Allen Blevins, Steve O'Brien,  Tinsley Carter, Wes Browne, Debbie Fickett-Wilbar, J.T. Gilbert, Katherine Bailey, Sam Davies, and  Cathy Howell all gave me ideas or stories.

In the broadcast world, the angelic Danielle Morgan and her cohorts at WYMT, Neil Middleton, and Steve Hensley have given me ideas and inspirations. Also, Tom Leach, Joe Elliott, Tad Murray, Mark Hebert, Kyle Sowers, Leland Conway, Ferrell Wellman, Renee Shaw, Scott Sloan, and Dave Baker have made me part of their shows as did the late "Cool Ghoul", Dick Von Hoene.

In the world of print, Keith Yarber, Ronnie Ellis, John Eckberg, Mark Neikirk, Carl West, Marisa Anders, Samantha Swindler, Jim Gaines, Ken Hart, and Randy Patrick are among those who have made a special effort to promote my syndicated newspaper column.

Bob and Shirley Sanders grew up in Covington, and Bob's parents were dear friends of my parents. They could write a better book than this one and their daughter Maria is a better writer than I could ever hope to be.

Al Smith is mentioned frequently in the book, but I cannot thank him and his wife, Martha Helen, enough for their undying friendship and love. Al is the role model for how I want to live the rest of my life. A lofty goal, but I am going to give it my best shot.

Al has helped me develop friendships with two of Kentucky's greatest broadcasting giants, O. Leonard (Len) Press and Ken Kurtz. Dinner with them is better than any graduate school journalism class.

Al Smith has mentored a ton of journalists but none more successful than Al Cross. Al Cross is a former national President of the Society of Professional Journalists and the greatest political writer in Kentucky's history.

Al Cross edited the introduction for this book with a red pen and fine tooth comb. The finished product shows his wisdom and editing prowess.

One last note on SPJ; I am Secretary for the Bluegrass (Kentucky) Chapter and my fellow board members like John Nelson, Ken Kurtz, Liz Hanson, Vanessa Gallman, Ferrell Wellman, Jack Brammer, and Laura Glasscock are great friends and sounding boards.

At the *Courier-Journal*, Byron Crawford is a friend who helps and encourages me and Tom Loftus keeps my ego in check. Stephanie Steitzer is a great source of information; David Hawpe is a great mind who inspires me; and John David Dyche gives me an intelligent man to argue and fight with.

Bobbie Ann Mason and Silas House are two Kentuckians who show that great writing and civic activism can go together.

Joe Nocera at the *New York Times* gives me ideas, encouragement, and inspiration. He is always one of the "Smartest Guys in the Room." He lost a bet to me and wore a white shirt on television. When he receives his long overdue Pulitzer Prize, I will wear something wild and crazy in his honor.

Although I mention them in the previous book, I have to thank again, Editor Jim Todd and the people at the *Richmond Register*. Jim is a good friend and a great man. It was the worst paper in Kentucky when he took over, and one year later the Kentucky Press Association voted it the best.

I feel like the *Register* staff are part of my family and appreciate what Publisher Nick Lewis and Associate Editor Lorie Love do to accommodate me.

I also want to mention former *Register* Associate Editors Jennifer Kustes Thornberry and Jodi Whitaker.

I misspelled Jennifer's name in my last book and hope I got it right this time. Jodi left the *Register* and became Press Secretary for Governor Ernie Fletcher. Jodi will be happy to know that Governor Fletcher's name does not appear in any chapter of this book.

I've never met or communicated with Gay Talese but went on a mission to read everything he has ever written. It was a worthwhile endeavor, and the format of his book, *Fame and Obscurity*, was an inspiration for this book.

I need to mention Jimmy Buffett. I frequently quote his songs, and my book title is a not so subtle reference to one of his biggest hits.

My father always encouraged me to be a writer, and he was disappointed when I stopped writing in the mid 1980's. He often told me, "If you write stories about my life, you will have a best seller."

I think dad may have been right.

# Don McNay: Author and Syndicated Columnist

Don McNay is an award winning author and syndicated columnist. He is the author of *The Unbridled World of Ernie Fletcher*. His business and social commentary columns appear in over 200 publications.

Along with his achievements in the literary world, McNay is one of the world's most successful structured settlement and "life transitions" consultants. He has worked with hundreds of injury victims, people who receive large lump sums, and lottery winners. He has four professional designations in the financial services industry.

McNay has Master's degrees from Vanderbilt University and the American College in Bryn Mawr, Pennsylvania. He is a graduate of Eastern Kentucky University and was inducted into the EKU Hall of Distinguished Alumni in 1998. He was named Outstanding Young Lexingtonian by the Lexington (Ky.) Jaycees in 1985.

Don has been featured in Forbes Magazine, The Lexington Herald Leader, The Courier Journal, The Cincinnati Enquirer, Registered Representative Magazine, and Financial Planning Magazine.

### Don McNay
don@donmcnay
www.donmcnay.com
122 North Second Street
Richmond, Ky. 40475
1-800-Mr. McNay
(859) 626-3633 (fax)

# Ollie and Theresa McNay Nursing Scholarship at Eastern Kentucky University

The book tells you a lot about my father and mother but I wanted to add a few words about my sister, Theresa.

Theresa died in October, 2006, due to an accidental fall. She was in good health, and it was completely unexpected.

Theresa and I had grown very close after my mother's death, which occurred six months before Theresa passed away. We discussed, almost daily, the completion of my first book, *The Unbridled World of Ernie Fletcher*. I was reading a very nice review of my book by David Hawpe, Editorial Director of the *Louisville Courier-Journal*, when I received the unexpected call about her death.

Theresa had just started her dream job as a chemical purchaser for Proctor and Gamble. Before that, she had worked as a gourmet chef, a food buyer, and a restaurant manager.

Her greatest pride was in her children, Nick and Lyndsay. After my mother's death, we were talking about a person's legacy. She said, "My legacy is my children. When you look at the tremendous children that I raised, I had to have done something right."

I certainly agree with her assessment. Nick and Lyndsay would make any parent proud. I am certainly proud to be their uncle.

When mom died, Theresa and I started a scholarship fund in mom's name at Eastern Kentucky University. When Theresa died, Nick and I decided to re-name the scholarship for both Ollie and Theresa.

The fund is set up to provide support each academic year to a nursing student who is also a single parent. Ideally, the student will be from Kenton County, Kentucky because that is where my mother and my sister lived almost all their lives.

All donations, large and small, are appreciated. We raised the $10,000 initially needed to endow the scholarship and the average donation was around $25.

You can send donations to:

The Ollie and Theresa McNay Nursing Scholarship,
EKU Foundation,
Eastern Kentucky University,
CPO 19A,
521 Lancaster Ave, Richmond, KY 40475

Eastern Kentucky University allows you to make donations via credit card.

Since mom was allegedly speaking to credit card company representatives well after her death, that may be the appropriate way to go.

If you donate online, please designate the Ollie and Theresa McNay Scholarship in the right corner as the recipient of your donation. Also, please note the McNay Scholarship on any check you submit. Please email me at don@donmcnay.com if you make a donation and I will track it and personally thank you.

# Praise for Don McNay and *The Unbridled World of Ernie Fletcher*

## www.unbridlederniefletcher.com

"Try this one. If you enjoy Kentucky politics as much as I do, you'll like it."

**—David Hawpe, Editorial Director, The (Louisville) Courier-Journal**

"Thank goodness there are still journalists like Don McNay left in Kentucky and America: fearless, truthful, compelling and willing to take on powerful interests. He's what the First Amendment was all about two centuries back. Do yourself a favor and buy this book."

**—John Eckberg, author of *Road Dog*; *The Success Effect*; and a business reporter at *The Cincinnati Enquirer***

Don McNay came to journalism relatively late, but he quickly proved that he has some attributes of fine journalists—a nose for news, a sense of justice, a capacity for outrage about injustice, a sympathy for the average person, a willingness to speak truth to power, and a sense of humor.

**—Al Cross, Director of the Institute for Rural Journalism and Community Issues, based at the University of Kentucky, and political writer for The (Louisville) Courier-Journal for 15 1/2 years.**

"The claimed accomplishments of a political leader can only be measured with good and accurate information, and the consistent reports of Don McNay certainly provide that reliable news."

**—Former Kentucky Governor Julian M. Carroll**

"Rock n' roll can parallel life and politics in ways that are funny, ironic, incisive, and profound and thus, Don McNay engages his readers. Lyrics from the likes of John Mellencamp and Melissa Etheridge spotlight McNay's tough topics, and McNay's research and plain-spoken style enlightens."

**—Suzette Martinez Standring, Immediate Past President, National Society of Newspaper Columnists**

"In rapid time, Don McNay has emerged as a powerful voice for disempowered Kentuckians: men and women who work hard and play by the rules, but whose quest for a share of the American Dream is frustrated by corrupt politicians and special interests. May his voice continue to resonate."

**—Jonathan Miller, Kentucky State Treasurer and author of *The Compassionate Community: Ten Values to Unite America***

"Thank God the SOB wasn't writing back when I ran for office."

**—Rick Robinson, Fort Mitchell attorney, former congressional aide and former congressional candidate.**

Some people like to go to the track and catch a race or to the stadium and watch nine innings. They go with a pencil behind their ear—and they keep notes. They may curse the stumbling horse or the third baseman's sloppy glove. But they curse them out of love, as a mother scolds a wayward child. Don McNay may love horses, he may love baseball. I honestly don't know. But I do know he loves politics, and he keeps notes. Like any true fan, his aspersions are from the heart. He only wants that horse to run like he did in the morning workout, that third baseman to catch like he did in the minors and that governor to govern the way he promised to in the campaign.

**—Mark Neikirk, Managing Editor of the Cincinnati Post and the Kentucky Post.**

"Don McNay's snappy writing is an always-too-brief joy to read, as he exercises his sharp wit on the proud and powerful, giving a practical and down-to-earth take on how political maneuverings and economic rumblings affect regular Kentuckians."

**—Jim Gaines, Political Reporter for the Bowling Green Daily News.**

"Don McNay knows Kentucky and isn't afraid to call 'em as he sees 'em—and have a good laugh at 'em as well."

**—Samantha Bennett, Columnist for the Pittsburgh Post-Gazette and Vice President of the National Society of Newspaper Columnists.**

"Don McNay is a keen observer of today's political, social, and economic landscape. He writes colorfully, clearly, and with great humor. But more than that, he exhibits the courage to speak the truth no matter the consequences. Such courage is a rare commodity in today's world."

**—Bill Garmer, Lexington Trial Attorney, Association of Trial Lawyers of America Governor and Former Chair of the Kentucky Democratic Party.**

"Don McNay is one of those fearless folks we all want to be. His writing is both wittingly disarming and courageously straight forward. McNay speaks and writes in a language we can all understand and never pulls punches. Taking on the establishment is easy; doing it with charm, style and clarity of reasoned thought makes for a very good read."

**—Alan Stein, President, Lexington Legends Professional Baseball Team.**

"I attended college with a special young man by the name of Don McNay. Don takes care of Fletcher, better than five million Republicans voting against him."

**—Carl Keith Greene, Columnist, Corbin Times Tribune.**

Printed in the United States
102244LV00001B/183/A

9 780979 364402